D1365320

JACK J. CALHOUN JR.

# the 12 INVESTMENT MYTHS

WHY INDIVIDUAL INVESTORS ARE
FAILING MISERABLY AND HOW YOU
CAN AVOID BEING ONE OF THEM

Robert D. Reed Publishers
P.O. Box 1992
Bandon, OR 97411
Phone: 541-347-9882; Fax: -9883
E-mail: 4bobreed@msn.com
Website: www.rdrpublishers.com

Editor: Zuzana Urbanek, Z-Ink.
Cover Designer: Gary Bannister, Farmhouse Design Studio
Typesetter: Mait Ainsaar, BICN Marketing & Design
Author photo: Trisha Addicks, Trisha Addicks Photography

ISBN: 978-1-934759-19-6

Library of Congress Control Number: 2008938996

Manufactured and Printed in the United States of America

To contact the author, write to: twelvemyths@hotmail.com

*For Nancy, Georgia and Tripp;*
*Wealth beyond measure…*

# ACKNOWLEDGMENTS

**This book would not** exist without the encouragement and direction of Steve Chandler – consultant, coach and writer extraordinaire. It has been a privilege to work with you, Steve! For my wife, Nancy, whose love for me and faith in me has been unwavering, I thank God every day. I am indebted to my father, Jack Calhoun Sr., who realized there was a right way and a wrong way to be in the investment business, chose the right way and then showed it to me. Many thanks to my mother, Marianne Craft, for her input and encouragement in this effort. To Dennis Covington, my business partner, who graciously indulges my writing habit and keeps the ship running smoothly, I offer this book as testimony that your faith was not in vain. To John McMillen, Kate Carlile, Macora Spann, Laura Taylor, Scott Pritchard and Stephanie Needham, incredible team members who accomplish incredible things for our firm.

To Frank Craft and Marcia Calhoun, I am grateful for three decades of loyalty, love and support. Thanks to Stewart Calhoun, Agie and Brad Rutkowski, Trisha Addicks, Dee Anne Sjogren, John Bowen, Jim Boulay and everyone who took the time to review the early drafts of this book; your insights were invaluable!

To the Addicks, the Asbills, the Covingtons, the Dunns, the Fogels, the Griders and the Novembers – friends who are family. Thanks to the entire Baldwin clan for welcoming me into your wonderful family, and for pretending to enjoy all the "Fun Facts from Uncle Jack".

Finally, many thanks to Bob Reed, Cleone Lyvonne and Mait Ainsaar for your expertise in taking my manuscript and making it a book.

*No one is too stupid to make money in the stock market. But there are many who are too smart to make money.*

**– Ben Stein, economist, author, actor, bon vivant**

# TABLE OF CONTENTS

# AUTHOR'S NOTE

**Throughout this book I** use the term "Wall Street" as a catch-all for the transactional side of the investment industry that plays to investors' emotions and encourages in them a destructive "trade first, think later" mentality. These institutions include certain brokerage firms, investment banks, retail banks, analysts and mutual-fund companies that are, in fact, scattered around the world.

# INTRODUCTION

**4.5%.**

That was the annual return for the average stock-fund investor for the 20-year period ending in 2007, according to a study by the respected research firm, Dalbar, Inc.[1] Not the return of the average stock fund, mind you, but the return of the average *investor* in stock funds.

*Four-point-five percent!*

Here's the really depressing part: The stock market's return (as measured by the S&P 500 index) during that same period of time was 11.81%. Even treasury bills earned a higher return than the average equity-fund investor. And this during one of the best runs in the stock market's history!

The market's investment return was there to be had. As Warren Buffet noted in Berkshire Hathaway's 2004 Annual Report:

*"Over the [past] 35 years, American business has delivered terrific results. It should therefore have been easy for investors to earn juicy returns: All they had to do was piggyback Corporate America in a diversified, low-expense way. An index fund that they never touched would have done the job. Instead many investors have had experiences ranging from mediocre to disastrous."* [2]

As Mr. Buffet notes, it was all there for the taking – all the return the market wanted to give. Investors, alas, declined the offer. It is as if someone is publishing the winning lottery numbers on the front page of the newspaper every day *but no one is picking them.*

As an investment advisor, I find this maddening. It stems, I believe, from a fundamental lack of understanding about the role human emotion plays in investing. People want to distill investing down to a purely analytical pursuit. This is akin to distilling football down to the forward advancement of an oblong spheroid. It might technically be true, but it wholly escapes the *emotion* of the thing. Grown men crying and hugging in public; babies being named after coaches; divorce decrees specifying which spouse gets the season tickets – *that* is the emotion of football. And emotion impregnates investing even more than the ol' pigskin. It goes to the core of our human instincts: to fear and greed, to prosperity and poverty, to comfort and anxiety. To survival and annihilation. If you think that's overly dramatic, consider yourself the lucky beneficiary of a prosperous age. It certainly wasn't so to the folks who lived through the Great Depression, who became this nation's thriftiest and most conservative group of investors ever, the stark fear of what they lived through still guiding their financial decisions three-quarters of a century later.

At the root of this lack of awareness and appreciation for the role of emotion in investing lies a collection of popular, and yet mistaken, beliefs – myths, as it were. These myths are widely propagated by the Wall Street hype machine and, by extension, the mass media, which relies on that hype machine for most of its content. At first blush, they are beliefs that seem quite logical. And this is what makes them so dangerous, because on closer examination they are the myths that cost investors billions of dollars each year. They are the myths that encourage emotional decision-making in investors.

The answer to these myths – the solution to the problem – is decidedly and deceptively simple. As you will note in the chapters that follow, the principles of successful investing are not complicated or mysterious; there are not even that many of them. The *adherence* to those principles, however, is another story entirely; it requires a Herculean effort to muster the discipline, courage, confidence and resolve required to stay the course *no matter the present market environment.* Even if everyone you know has put all their money in tech stocks. Even if the market has dropped twenty percent in a month, as it did in October 2008. Even if the World Trade Center has just been destroyed right before your eyes.

This book, then, is devoted to helping you, the investor, discern the fallacies about investing that Wall Street, the media and your friends and neighbors throw at you on a daily basis. To recognize them when you hear them, remember why they are wrong, and know what to do about them. To challenge you to face the fact that controlling your emotions, your behavior, is really what is by far going to determine whether you amass enough money to sustain you through what will likely be a very long retirement.

In short, to avoid being part of the investing masses who – needlessly and perpetually – leave all that money on the table.

– J.C.

# MYTH 1

*"I can be just as dumb as anyone else."* [3]
*– Peter Lynch, famed former manager of Fidelity's Magellan fund,*
*when asked to explain his long-running infatuation*
*with Fannie Mae stock after it cratered*

**My wife has several** qualities about her that I found very desirable when we were in our courting phase. First, of course, is her sheer physical beauty and keen intellect (I did not just fall off the turnip truck here). But she also had two other things going for her that I thought made her great marriage material: She had two older brothers, and she was a kindergarten teacher.

I knew that these things were great preparation for life with a man. Living with older brothers for almost two decades had well acquainted her with the male standard of decorum and personal hygiene (i.e., the complete lack thereof). And spending thirty hours a week trying to

1

reason with five-year-olds was great training for the male level of emotional maturity.

In essence, my wife's expectations about men had been "pre-lowered", and I knew I was just the man to meet those expectations. I also knew this would save me a lot of hard work during the early years of our marriage.

Interestingly, those same attributes my wife possessed – patience, practicality, realistic expectations – are qualities that are also central to investment success. When you survey the landscape of investment alternatives, there will always be a few Fabios out there – hot funds and hot managers that have posted positively sexy returns. And, just like Fabio, they are not representative of reality. They are phantoms, flashes in the pan, and if you try to build a stable investment life around them they'll burn you every time.

But the index fund – well, Mr. Index Fund may not be sexy, sitting over there doing the dishes in his bowtie and black, horn-rimmed glasses. But he's going to get up every day and go to work and get the job done. He's not going to fool around, and he's not going to go chasing after the next hot thing. He's someone you can build a long-term relationship with, however boring and predictable that relationship might be.

This is investors' great Achilles heel – falling for the siren song of the hot fund instead of opting for the plodding efficiency of the index fund. There you are, innocently thumbing through, say, *Money* magazine in the examination room at your doctor's office. You come across an article that has a headline something like, "Five Funds for All Seasons", wherein are profiled five funds that have managed to post extraordinary returns, year in and year out, in markets both good and bad. The article carries glowing profiles of each fund's manager, including grand, portrait-style photos in which the manager undoubtedly has his arms folded across his chest and an earnest-yet-humble look on his face that seems to say: "All those who want to beat the market... *follow me!*"

Now, you are a rational person, and you know anything that looks too good to be true probably is. (You've told your children this many times, so you must believe it.) But there it is in full color right in front of you – the fund magician who has found the secret formula, the no-risk, no-worry path to riches. And so your greedy little ego begins to jump around in the back of your consciousness, thrusting its hand in the air and shouting, "Me! Me! I want to beat the market! I want some of that action!" So you tear out the article as quietly as you can and stuff it in your back pocket, resolved to call a discount broker when you get home and hop aboard this money train!

If you've ever done this, I'll bet you next month's mortgage payment your hot fund didn't continue to be so hot once you got into it. You probably arrived too late and caught the fund as it returned back to earth, posting so-so returns for the next few years until you got bored with it and went looking for the next Mr. Highreturn.

Investors make this mistake over and over, and it's easy to understand why. A logical, thinking person would assume that other logical, thinking people who are experts at investing should be able to beat the market. And yet – here's the kicker – *they don't.* In truth the majority of professional money managers – historically between 70% and 90% over ten-year time periods – do not beat their market benchmarks.

How can this be?

The answer lies within. The very fact that so much money is now being managed by professional investment managers via mutual funds, pension funds, hedge funds, endowments, etc., means that there are very few naïve investors in the marketplace, at least as far as the end-decision maker is concerned. And that means there aren't many opportunities to be had, because everyone already knows about them and the market has beaten a path to their door.

It hasn't always been this way. Fifty years ago, investors largely made their own investment decisions, calling in their stock picks to brokers who were little more than glorified order takers. People owned a scant handful of stocks – a dozen was a lot – almost all of which were blue chips, and then they acted in a prudent, conservative fashion and left the money alone to grow.

In those days, most of the trading volume on Wall Street was controlled by individual investors, and in such an environment professional investment managers had a lot of opportunity to add value. Information was sketchy and moved at a glacial pace compared to today's wired world. Professionals had access to pertinent knowledge that small investors could never access. Small cap and midcap stocks were virtual unknowns to most investors and presented a great opportunity for the professional. Insider tips and tidbits were shared among the Wall Street elite with near impunity, and it was certainly possible – even probable – to beat the market through diligent research, skill, chicanery or some combination thereof.

Suffice it to say, those days are gone. Today few investors are brave (or foolhardy) enough to stake their life savings on a half-dozen stocks they picked on their own, typically turning over the stock-selection process to a mutual-fund manager, pension manager, etc. As a result, institutional investors control more than 85% of the trading volume in the market. By some estimates, the average large-cap stock is analyzed more than 200,000 times *per week*.

This, then, is the plight of today's professional money managers. It's not that they aren't smart people; it's that the opportunities are simply not there. There are no secrets to exploit, no rubes to take advantage of. The market has evolved (devolved?) into a universe of MBAs, all armed with the same information, analyzing relentlessly, trading furiously, trying to justify the fees they charge investors to beat the market. Ironically, the result of all this activity in an efficient market is that most managers – no matter how smart or well-intentioned they may be – end up trailing the market because the costs associated with their trading make that underperformance inevitable, a mathematical certainty. It's like giving a sculptor a completed masterpiece to work with; every move he makes is only going to do harm. It's a no-win proposition.

Ah, but hope springs eternal for the investor. *What about Peter Lynch?* you say. *What about Warren Buffett? What about Bill Miller? Market beaters one and all!*

To which I would say: Is that all you got?

In the investment industry, there are over 8,000 mutual funds (not counting share classes). More than 16,000 independent registered investment advisors. More than 200,000 stockbrokers. So why is it that when people search for examples of expert managers who have trounced the market over the years, they struggle to come up with more than a half-dozen examples? One would expect blind luck to yield more market-beating managers than that.

Here's another problem: Of the group that does beat the market, how can you really know if they were good or just lucky? In 2006, three noted professors published a groundbreaking study in which they applied established scientific methods to determine whether market-beating mutual funds had clearly bested the market by skill, as opposed to luck. Their conclusion? The number of fund managers who had beaten the market in such a convincing manner that it could only be attributed to skill was 0.6% – essentially zero![4]

In assessing the implications of that study, *New York Times* columnist Mark Hulbert noted: "There was once a small number of fund managers with genuine market-beating abilities, as judged by having past performance so good that their records could not be attributed to luck alone. But virtually none remain today. Index funds are the only rational alternative for almost all mutual fund investors, according to the study's findings."[5]

Look at this from another perspective. Let's say that you gathered 8,000 of your closest friends together (clearly you're very social) and asked them each to pick 100 stocks. Then you tracked your friends' portfolios over a ten-year period, at the end of which you ranked them from best to worst. There at the top, most assuredly, would be one of your friends – probably a couple dozen of your friends, actually – who had dramatically outperformed the market. You rush to congratulate your buddy at the top, who has posted positively stratospheric returns, and tell him you want him to manage your money.

"But I didn't know what I was doing!" your friend protests. "You just told me to pick 100 stocks, so I did. I don't even know how I did this – I was just lucky!"

No matter, you say – the numbers speak for themselves. You then arrange a photo shoot for your friend with *Forbes* magazine (arms crossed, of course) and get him a cover story with the headline "America's Newest Fund Superstar!"

Is it fair to compare super-smart, MBA-laden fund managers with a lucky monkey who backed into stellar returns? It may seem a ridiculous comparison, but it's not entirely off the mark. The famed Bill Miller himself, manager of the Legg Mason Value Trust fund that beat the S&P 500 for 15 consecutive years, admitted as much. In his fund's Fourth Quarter 2005 shareholder letter, Mr. Miller, with refreshing candor, said the following:

*You are probably aware that the Legg Mason Value Trust has outperformed the S&P 500 index for each of the past 15 calendar years. That may be the reason you decided to purchase the fund. If so, we are flattered, but believe you are setting yourself up for disappointment. While we are pleased to have performed as we have, our so-called "streak" is a fortunate accident of the calendar. Over the past 15 years, the December-to-December time frame is the only one of the twelve-month periods where our results have always outpaced those of the index. If your expectation is that we will outperform the market every year, you can expect to be disappointed.*[6]

Whoa. Three cheers for Mr. Miller's honesty, for rare is the successful active manager who will admit that luck had as much to do as skill with a long run of market-beating performance. (I'm sure the Legg

Mason P.R. department was less excited about his candor.) And perhaps Mr. Miller is clairvoyant after all, because the next year his fund's long hot streak came to an end. In 2006 the Legg Mason Value Trust fund gained 5.9%, underperforming the S&P 500 by nearly 10%. (The truth is that it is unfair to benchmark a value fund to the S&P 500, but that didn't stop the media from crowning Mr. Miller's fund as king for the decade it was trouncing that index.)

And let's be honest about Warren Buffett. He's not so much an investor as an acquirer. He buys large stakes in companies (or, often, the whole company) and then takes an active role in their management and corporate governance. He's a genius at this, and his accolades are well deserved, but he's hardly representative of a money manager sitting at a computer, picking stocks and trying to beat the market. In fact, as noted in the introduction, Mr. Buffett is an ardent advocate of index funds for individual investors.

For investors, this may be the hardest thing to let go of – the unrelenting desire to find the market-beating guru and ride his or her genius to riches. After all, if the race always goes to the swiftest runner, why shouldn't we expect the investment riches to go to the smartest investor?

Here's the thing: the investment riches *do* go to the smartest investor. But we need to clarify what, exactly, we mean by "smart," and we need to clarify just what game it is we are playing.

There is some debate among intellectuals as to exactly how "efficient" the stock market is at setting prices. But there is very little debate about the notion that the market is extremely efficient at making investors wealthy over time. It is therefore not a wise use of our money to engage in a long-running pursuit of finding the needle-in-the-haystack fund manager whose goal it is to prove, essentially, that the market *doesn't* work.

Smart investors, then, are those who strive to use the markets to their fullest advantage. They want to get out of their own way – by not moving around, by not succumbing to their emotions, and by not driving up fees and expenses – so that the market can work its long-term magic. They want to use investment vehicles that reflect this belief. And they want to use an investment advisor who embraces this belief.

The name of the game is "let's *use* the market," not "let's *beat* the market."

Don't let anyone – especially yourself – convince you otherwise.

## MYTH 1: A Savvy Investor Should Be Able to Beat the Market

FACT: Hope springs eternal for investors that they can find the market-beating guru to lead them to easy riches. But active managers have a nearly insurmountable hurdle to overcome due to the high costs associated with frequent trading. Those few managers who beat their benchmark are usually flashes in the pan and don't sustain their winning ways for long. Investors who fall prey to the siren song of the market-beating guru usually end up experiencing only disappointment and lost potential earnings as they migrate from one high-flyer to another just as the managers are poised for a return to mediocre performance.

SOLUTION: Learn to joyously accept the fact that the market is your friend to be embraced, not an enemy to be vanquished. Earning market rates-of-return is hardly accepting "average" returns, because historically the market beats more than 80% of active managers.

# MYTH 2

*"Your job is to turn your clients' net worth into your own."*
*— Blaine Lourd, former stockbroker,*
*quoting advice a fellow broker gave him in*
*his early days in the industry, in Portfolio.com magazine.*

**My father started out** in the investment business more than thirty years ago, a rookie stockbroker freshly scrubbed and full of enthusiasm, ready to make money for (1) his clients, (2) himself and (3) his firm.

It took about two years, he says, for him to realize that the firm didn't much care about the first two.

Dad's tale of woe began the very first week, when he was told to provide a list of friends and relatives on whom he would be required to call. He was given a list of products to be sold – oil and gas partnerships, variable annuities, thirty-year bonds, hot new IPOs, etc. – and production targets for each of them. Then he was told to start dialing for dollars.

9

Initially Dad thought this was just the way it worked in the industry. His clients needed investments and Dad had access to plenty of investments to sell them. But over time, my father began to awaken to a fundamental reality about the way things were being run in the brokerage industry: As a general rule, the firms were making tons of money, and the investors were, um...*not*. This inescapable truth so gnawed at Dad that he finally went into business for himself as a fee-only, independent investment advisor where there was no product that had to be sold and no bosses to tell him who to sell it to.

That particular scenario played out nearly three decades ago, but in the intervening years it has been repeated many times in many forms with many millions of unwitting investors. From spurious annuities to speculative dot-com stocks to the outright fraud of letting market timers make billions in profits at the expense of their fund shareholders, Wall Street's list of transgressions against individual investors is long and sordid.

It reached its zenith in the fall of 2008, when Wall Street's oldest and largest investment banks were undone by their own hand, victims of the toxic mortgage-backed derivatives they created and ultimately kept on their own books. It is no small irony that after decades of blowing up their clients' portfolios, Wall Street's big boys finally blew up *themselves*. Rest assured, however, that while the Wall Street old guard has been forced to change its stripes, its culture remains very much intact.

Why are things this way, you ask? Why does this pattern seem to repeat itself time after time with this country's biggest brokerage firms – with the individual investor being left holding the bag? The unvarnished truth is that, despite what their glitzy brochures and gauzy ad campaigns want you to believe, brokerage firms are *not* built on a client service model. They are built on a *product distribution* model. This is a key distinction and the root of the problem, at least as it relates to you.

On the one hand, brokerage houses are the primary facilitators of the global capital markets. They underwrite initial public stock offerings.

They coordinate mergers and acquisitions. They structure massive debt offerings for major corporations. Essentially they are the oil that lubes the gears of the world's financial markets. For this, we salute them.

But this is also where the *product* gets created. For example, when brokerage firms participate in the underwriting of an initial public stock offering (IPO), they have to buy huge positions in the stock themselves. Essentially, they become stock wholesalers. So now they have two big reasons to get the stock sold at the highest price possible – one, to appease their important new investment banking client they just took public; and, two, because they now own a large chunk of the stock themselves and they need to, well, *unload* it.

So…who to unload it upon? The individual investor! (The picture is getting clearer, isn't it?) In the eyes of the brokerage industry – and I am referring to the executives at the very top of the industry – individual investors are the *consuming public*. They are viewed just the same way the CEO of Procter & Gamble views them; as the masses who buy the product.

This is all well and good when you're buying, say, canned soup. It is easy for you, the consumer, to evaluate your options based on what the label says and how the soup tastes. If you find that you made a bad choice, you're only out two bucks, and now you'll know better the next time you go to the grocery store.

Contrast this with the "consumer's" experience at the brokerage firm. You don't have labels to compare, you have prospectuses that are about as reader-friendly as the U.S. tax code. And you're not buying a can of soup; often you're being urged to buy a complex investment such as an annuity, with draconian surrender charges and severe tax consequences waiting for you if you change your mind and want to get out.

Meanwhile, your only meaningful information about the merits of this investment comes from – surprise! – the broker who gets paid to sell you the product. (This is akin to asking the Anheuser Busch sales rep about the merits of Budweiser.) And, unlike the soup consumer, the poor soul who makes a bad investment choice can very quickly find himself out his life savings.

The root of this problem lies in the very nature of the brokerage industry itself. Brokerage firms can't change what they are on the one side – the facilitators (brokers) of the global capital markets – and so they can't change what they are on the other side, which is the distributor of the product that gets created as a result of their brokerage activities. If brokerage firms start getting overly concerned about doing what is solely in your best interest – diversify using low-cost investments, minimize trading activity, etc. – then the machine will break down. They must create the demand among individual investors, or there will be no need for the supply generated from their investment banking activities. And what kind of awful world would *that* be?

Brokerage firms want you to believe they can wear the two hats of Product Distribution and Client Service simultaneously, but such an effort is inherently contradictory. You can't serve both of those masters; when you favor one side, it is going to be at the expense of the other. And above all, what brokerage firms can *never, ever* afford to do is jeopardize the deal flow from their investment banking activities; if they did, they would be out of business in very short order. If a brokerage firm suddenly got a pang of conscience and started telling investors that, well, they probably don't want to buy the stock of that company that they just helped take public – do you think that company is going to let the brokerage firm in on any new offerings in the future? And what would happen to all that dubious stock the firm has sitting on its own books?

This is the dirty little secret of the brokerage industry, the one that keeps causing it to incur billions of dollars in fines. The one they really don't want you focusing on. So the glossy ad campaigns pay lip service to a client-service model while, internally, the entire focus is on pushing product, product, product. They develop elaborate training programs for their broker sales forces to teach them how to sell that product. They establish "production bonuses." They have contests for luxury cruises based on "production." They put their top "producers" in corner offices and run the poor "producers" out of the firm all together. In short, they create a macho culture (even for women) where selling product is king, and the interests of the client are – we are being charitable here – secondary.

My father's take on this culture is informing. He says that, as a rookie stockbroker, you are immersed in this mentality from the minute you walk in the door of the wirehouse. They spoon-feed you their worldview about how to sell product and overwhelm you with information and put you on a phone dialing for dollars all within the first week. You are encouraged to start with friends and family since they make the easiest targets – er, prospects. Your production is tracked and is known by all and if you aren't producing they do not stand idly by. They hover over you, wanting to know why you are lagging behind the others and what you intend to do about it. If you don't start producing in short order you are shown the door.

The training programs are all designed to make the brokers feel like they are learning about the fundamentals of successful investing. The trainers speak of financial planning and diversification and taking care of the client. But behind the curtain lies the wizard – the executives at the top who never lose site of the fact that they've got product that has got to be sold. It is a driving need that infuses the entire organization.

This is how so many investors end up with what we at our firm call "Broker Gumbo" – a portfolio that has a little bit of everything thrown in it. Brokers are "encouraged" by their bosses to favor certain products, and that encouragement shows up in the investor's portfolio over time. You've got five or six mutual funds, usually the brokerage firm's proprietary "house" funds; you've got a handful of stocks; you've got a couple of variable annuities; you've got a few long-term bonds. And you've got absolutely zero game plan. There is no sense of managing the total portfolio, only of being presented every few months with yet another "opportunity."

Many such investors saw their net worth cut in half, or worse, during the 2000-02 bear market. They had been minding their own business, taking their broker's advice, assuming their best interests were being looked after. And because the growth style of investing was hot, the broker took the easy path and recommended lots of growth funds and growth stocks. There was probably an Internet fund, maybe a large chunk in Cisco or Intel. A few of the flashy dot-com stocks. And, rest assured, there weren't any value funds or REIT funds and probably not even any foreign funds in the portfolio, all of which had greatly underperformed growth stocks (so why try to sell any of *those*). A growth-heavy portfolio like that would have posted fabulous returns for quite a while, leading the investor to question the broker's recommendations less and less. And then it would have lost around sixty or seventy percent during the bear market that followed.

We saw a great many such investors walk through our door during those years, distressed and desperate for help. It was eye-opening to me during that time that the primary complaint was not about the losses, although, rest assured, the investors weren't happy about them. The primary complaint, the thing that we heard time and again, was this: "I don't understand what I'm invested in or why I'm in it. And I don't think my broker does either."

That was when the chickens came home to roost for the brokerage industry. According to a study conducted by The Spectrem Group, an independent research firm that tracks the habits of affluent investors, the brokerage industry saw its market share of wealthy investors fall by almost 50% from 2002 to 2004.[7] Here's the kicker: These affluent investors didn't go from one brokerage firm to another; they left the brokerage industry entirely, opting instead for independent advisory firms.

Such Registered Investment Advisors, or RIAs, as they are known, are governed by their respective state or, when large enough, the Securities & Exchange Commission. (Full disclosure: I am a principal in one such RIA.) RIAs have none of the sales pressure that brokers have, because there is no one breathing down their neck to push "product" on their clients, and because they cannot accept commissions. An RIA's only commodity is the quality of his or her advice and service. Advisors who go this route take on considerably more risk than do stockbrokers, because they are bound to a fiduciary standard of care, meaning that they are obligated to put the interests of their clients first, ahead of their own.

This is a key distinction, one that is lost on the great majority of individual investors. Being a fee-only RIA doesn't guarantee an advisor knows what he's doing, but it does provide one very important assurance for the investor: *Objectivity*. When there is no product being sold, there is no hidden agenda, no ulterior motive. That prevents the sort of abuses outlined at the beginning of this chapter, because there is no incentive to engage in them. Why would I want to buy and sell every stock in your portfolio over and over again if I don't have any financial incentive to do so? Why would I want to sell you a fund that has an egregiously high expense ratio if I'm not being paid part of the proceeds?

The obvious answer is that I wouldn't. In fact, for a fee-based advisor, engaging in such behavior is detrimental both to the client and himself, because excess trading and high fund fees will drag down the investor's return, which reduces the investor's assets, which lowers the advisor's fee.

See how nicely those interests all line up?

## MYTH 2: Brokerage Firms Are Built on a Client Service Model

FACT: The big brokerage firms are not built on a client-service model; they are built on a *product-distribution* model. The endless, massive fines those firms keep incurring for violating their investors' best interests testify to this fact. Brokers who are compensated by the products they sell cannot claim to be objective and do not meet a fiduciary standard of care for their clients.

SOLUTION: If you want to work with an advisor, find one who is an independent, fee-only Registered Investment Advisor. Such RIAs cannot accept commissions and act as fiduciaries for their clients, meaning they are required to put their clients' best interests ahead of their own.

# MYTH 3

## It's All about Performance

*"If past history was all there was to the game, the richest people would be librarians."*

**– Warren Buffett**

**I know what you're** thinking. It's the same thing almost all investors are thinking.

*It's all about performance.*

Prepare to be amazed, then, when I tell you this:

It is NOT about performance.

Now you are thinking I am a complete idiot. Let me explain...

It is true that obtaining good performance from your investments is desirable and necessary. No argument there. But when investors *focus* on performance, *pursue* performance, make decisions *based* on performance, they usually end up getting *bad* performance.

Ironic, isn't it?

Successful investing is full of seemingly logical contradictions such as this, which is why most investors fail to succeed. It just goes against our rational nature to believe that you shouldn't base your evaluation of an investment on something so clearly pertinent as its prior performance history.

The problem is, it isn't pertinent. An investment's past performance – be it stock, fund or money manager – is really just that. *Past* performance. A mutual fund that has enjoyed a great run for the past five years tells you only that it would have been nice to have been in the fund. And, since you weren't, what does it matter?

There has never been a single verifiable study that has found a connection between past performance and future performance. Not one. If there was, rest assured, the world would beat a path to that connection and it would be arbitraged away forthwith.

Conversely, there is a great deal of supporting data that proves the opposite to be true – that there is *no* connection between past and future performance. One recent analysis was conducted by Standard & Poor's, Inc. In its 2006 "Mutual Fund Persistence Scorecard," the company found that only 17.3% of large-cap funds with a top-quartile ranking over the five years ending December 31, 2001, maintained a top-quartile ranking over the next five years ending December 31, 2006. Meanwhile, only 10.4% of midcap funds and 17.7% of small-cap funds maintained a top-quartile performance over the same period.[8]

Assessing the results of their study, Standard & Poor's concluded that "research suggests that screening for top-quartile funds, as the sole basis for an investment decision, is inappropriate. Very few funds repeat a top-quartile performance."[9]

To put it bluntly – picking winners is a waste of time. It has as much correlation to future success as picking funds based on the manager's shoe size. It turns out the ubiquitous disclaimer that the SEC requires investment professionals to put on sales materials *"Past performance does not guarantee future results"* is not really a disclaimer at all. It's the stone cold truth.

Alas, this disclaimer is treated as mere legalese by the investment industry, buried in fine print at the bottom of the ad, while the real message it wants investors to get – PERFORMANCE – is in ninety-point type at the top. The intent of the investment provider's message is clear: "Don't worry so much about the disclaimer; that's just what the government stiffs make us say. *Focus on the juice!*"

Performance is the easiest sales job in the investment industry. It is so painfully simple to find a list of hot mutual funds and then build a story around it. Just run a simple filter in any mutual-fund database – Morningstar, Value Line, etc. – for top performers for both five- and ten-year time periods and – *boom* – the software spits out your list and you've got your sales story. That story usually goes something like this:

"Well, Mrs. Butterworth, my firm's research department has done some extensive, um, research. And they've come up with this 'Focus List' of funds that have had just outstanding performance."

"Sounds good," says Mrs. Butterworth. "Tell me more."

"Well, each of these funds has a rating of five horseshoes."

"*Horseshoes?*"

"Yes, well, Morningstar already took the star symbol, and Value Line took diamonds. We thought clovers and moons sounded too much like Lucky Charms cereal, so our marketing department went with horseshoes."

"I'm sorry I asked," says Mrs. Butterworth.

"Anyway, these funds have all been top performers. Just the tops. Now, if you'll just sign here we'll get the account open for you…"

And this, unfortunately, is where Mrs. Butterworth and nearly all other investors do as they are sold and sign the forms. Because the clear implication is that these top performers of the past will continue to be top performers in the future.

Oh, how I wish it were so. If it were, the title of this book would be something like, "HOW YOU CAN USE MY EXCLUSIVE STAR-

RATING SYSTEM TO BEAT THE MARKET!" and I would be writing to you from my private island in the Bahamas.

It is not only not true, it is a dangerous game to play. Over long periods of time – ten years or more – the performance difference between the top quartile and bottom quartile funds in the same category will be pretty slim, usually just a few percentage points. In the short-term, however, the performance of individual funds within these categories will bounce around quite a bit. So funds that have had unusually good performance are very often poised for what statisticians call "reversion to the mean" – a downward tumble that, when averaged with the earlier period of very good performance, will put the fund right where one would expect it, which is in line with other funds within its category.

The trouble is, you, the investor, weren't there for the earlier period of very good performance. The broker is selling you on that period and has you believing that you are joining a very exclusive party. But the truth is that you are more likely arriving late, as the party guests are stumbling out the door, just in time for the cops to show up.

If you want to know how cynical the investment industry really is about hyping performance, look no further than a concept known as an "incubator fund." Sounds bizarre, but the concept is quite simple: Large mutual-fund companies, all of which have a huge staff of managers at their disposal, will assign, say, five managers the task of starting a new fund. But these five funds won't yet be offered to the investing public; they are being treated as "experimental" funds that the mutual-fund company is in the process of "developing" to see how the different managers' methodologies work out – incubating them, as it were.

After a year or two, odds being what they are, one of the new funds likely will have posted outstanding returns, well ahead of the others. At this point, the fund company steps in, shuts down the other funds that lagged behind, takes the hot manager who shot the lights out and rolls the fund out to the marketplace. Here's the kicker: *the fund company can legally claim, and thus promote, the returns that the manager generated while running his fund in its "incubation" period.* Now the fund company has its coveted "five-star" fund, virtually assuring that millions of dollars will flow into it, without ever having to disclose the little internal experiment it conducted wherein it simply played the odds to back into a hot fund. Meanwhile, the investors who flow into the fund will very likely find that these exceptional returns don't persist and, as in the prior example, arrive just in time for the ride back down to reality.

It's not as if the mutual-fund company isn't aware of this; it simply doesn't allow itself to really *think* about it (some might call this a "lack of conscience"). Instead, it focuses on keeping investors jumping around within its different funds, trying to get them to chase the next hot thing. In the investment business this is known as "chasing returns"; it is the easiest sell in the world, and it is a complete sham. But investors *want* to believe it; they want to believe that high-flying investments will continue to fly high. And the fund industry, being hugely overpopulated and facing stiff competition, has become extraordinarily adept at selling it to them.

Remember what all those TV and print ads for mutual-fund companies were selling back in 1999 and early 2000? Tech funds. And what would have been the worst possible thing to do with your money at that time? (*Hint*: tech funds!) Then, when the bubble burst and tech-fund investors lost somewhere around 80% of their money, what were the ads in 2002 trying to get investors to buy? Bond funds. And what would have been the worst possible thing to do with your money at that time? (*Hint*: bond funds!)

The table on the next page shows just how effective Wall Street was during that time at cajoling investors to move their money around by focusing on short-term performance. It shows the flow of cash into the various mutual-fund categories (ranked from most aggressive to least aggressive) from 1998 through 2002.

| Mutual Fund Inflows by Investment Objective, 1998-2002 (in millions) | | | | | |
|---|---|---|---|---|---|
|  | 1998 | 1999 | 2000 | 2001 | 2002 |
| Aggressive Growth | $11,664 | $ 34,340 | $ 129,327 | $ 19,015 | $ (1,079) |
| Growth | $64,255 | $ 97,002 | $ 119,079 | $ (1,836) | $ (25,066) |
| International | $ 831 | $ 5,987 | $ 31,523 | $ (21,802) | $ 5,535 |
| Growth & Income | $61,894 | $ 30,661 | $ (31,982) | $ 31,986 | $ 8,450 |
| Income | $ 4,864 | $ (14,509) | $ (19,056) | $ 4,565 | $ 3,561 |
| Balanced Funds | $10,154 | $ (12,352) | $ (31,784) | $ 9,520 | $ 9,212 |
| Bond Funds | $74,610 | $ (5,534) | $ (48,599) | $ 87,704 | $ 140,372 |

*Source: Investment Company Institute*

Note that in the pre-tech bubble year of 1998, cash flows into the mutual-fund categories were fairly well diversified. Then, in 1999, as dot-com mania began to sweep the land, note how all of the new dollars were flowing into the most aggressive segments of the market, while dollars invested in the more conservative fund categories were flowing out at lightning speed. This trend reached its zenith in 2000, when nearly every investable dollar controlled by individuals was flowing into the most aggressive, tech-heavy funds – at the worst possible time.

By the end of 2000, the Internet-stock bubble had burst, and the market began its long slide downward. By 2002, as the table shows, the vast majority of individual investors had fled the market for bond funds, assuring that they would miss the huge, four-year-long stock rally that began in March 2003. Thus, an investor who followed this lead would have incurred massive losses in the 2000-02 market crash and then been sitting on the sidelines in bond funds when stocks began their dramatic recovery. *No matter,* the mutual-fund company whispers in your ear – *just check out the returns of our REIT fund!*

This is the classic malaise that afflicts individual investors; forever buying high and selling low. It is how we get to the statistic mentioned in the introduction to this book, in which investor performance trails the stock market's performance by a huge margin over time. It is how people lose their life savings in the stock market and become convinced that "stocks" are the problem, when really their behavior is the problem – the endless pursuit of performance.

*The Economist* magazine of London ran an amusing story in 2000[10] highlighting the negative effects of this type of behavior. The article compared the investment results of two hypothetical investors during the twentieth century: Harry Hindsight and Felicity Foresight. Beginning January 1, 1900, with $1, Harry Hindsight engaged in typical investor behavior, throwing all of his money at the end of each year into whatever market sector had been hottest that year. Meanwhile, Felicity Foresight, possessed of a magical vision, started with the same $1 but put all of her money into the *coming year's* hottest asset class.

At the end of the twentieth century, Harry Hindsight's dollar had grown to $783. In comparison, had he invested in the broad stock market and left it alone, his dollar would have been worth $9,000 by the end of 1999.

And what of Felicity Foresight, who magically knew where to put her money in advance every year? What was her dollar worth at the end of 1999? (Bet you don't get it…)

$9,600,000,000,000,000,000.

That's $9.6 quintillion, in case you, like me, don't know what to call a number that has seventeen zeros in it. (For the record, after expenses were factored in, Felicity was only worth a few quadrillion dollars.)

This tells us two things. First, chasing performance is a complete waste of time; if you succumb to this temptation you will very likely end up doing much worse than the market. It also tells us something else very interesting – that if *anyone* was successfully chasing performance then Bill Gates would be doing their laundry and Warren Buffet would be answering the front door for them. And if you do a quick scan of the Forbes 400 list of this country's wealthiest individuals, you will note that "return chaser" is not among the occupations listed for any of them.

So if not performance…then what? If you want a very good way to pick a mutual fund that will outperform its peers, then focus on three things: sales charges, expense ratio, and turnover ratio. These criteria are easy to learn about, and they will have a very meaningful impact on a fund's future performance.

The part about sales charges is very easy: if a fund has them, don't buy it. It's really that simple. It doesn't matter if it's front loads, deferred loads, 12b-1 fees, or whatever. If a fund has different share classes with different sales charges – A shares, B shares, C shares, etc. – then you're talking to the wrong people. If there were no other options in this world, then perhaps it would be meaningful to spend time deciding if it's better to give up 5% of your money on the front end or be trapped in an investment for five years for fear of paying a back-end load. But with 8,000-plus funds out there, why should you have to make such an onerous deal with the devil?

*Run, Forrest, run!*

The expense ratio is a different story, because all funds have operating expenses they must cover. The question is, how much are they going to ding you, the shareholder, to cover those expenses? This is where index funds have a huge advantage; because they are passively managed funds that seek only to track a certain market index, they don't pay hefty fees to managers whose job it is to try to beat that index. Thus most index funds and ETFs have fees that are often more than 1% below the typical actively managed retail mutual fund.

Finally, the turnover ratio tells you how much trading is going on in the fund. It is a reflection of the annual percentage of the fund's stock portfolio that is "turned over" (sold off) during the year. Essentially, if a fund has a turnover ratio of 75%, then you can expect three out of four stocks that the fund holds today to not be there this time next year. Every time the fund sells a stock it pays a brokerage commission, and those commissions are considered to be operating expenses that come out of the fund, which lowers the returns to the shareholders. On top of this, stocks that are sold for gains trigger capital-gains taxes, adding an even greater expense burden on taxable investors in the fund.

Funds that keep expenses low and trading to a minimum will deliver a much higher after-tax return to their investors, thus starting them off well ahead of their high-fee, trade-happy peers. In a market that is highly efficient, such a hurdle is difficult to overcome. Thus do these measures tell you a lot more about the future success of a mutual fund than star ratings and hot-fund lists.

If you apply these criteria to the universe of retail mutual funds, you will be shocked at how quickly the list of 8,000 gets whittled down to just a few dozen. The fact is, such seemingly logical practices as controlling fees and taxes are exceedingly rare in the fund world, where "prudence" is a code word for "boring." And, as we've discussed, it is the retail fund industry's great need and desire to pump up the volume and get you drunk on the performance hooch, so that they can get you to buy, buy, buy and then sell, sell, sell and then buy, buy, buy some more.

This is equally true with the multitude of "separate account manager" programs the brokerage firms have cooked up in recent years, in which the firms sub-contract with private money managers in all sorts of categories and create a platform for their broker sales force to use. They tell you a story about how you – lucky you – now have access to primo money managers that ordinarily would have been available only to the Rockefellers and such. They tout the performance of these managers for all time periods, short and long, and rest assured every single manager in the program has had positively stellar returns.

The story may be shaded a little differently than the five-star mutual-fund spiel, but rest assured the results are the same. There is no way to use a money manager's prior performance to project how that manager will do going forward. It is merely an easy sales tool for the brokerage firm, because (again) investors *want* to believe it. Just as with the five-star funds mentioned above, investors who sign up for one of these manager programs usually find that the high-flying money managers do not continue to be so hot going forward. When that happens the brokerage firms will replace the underperforming managers with the latest crop of high performers, so that they can keep selling the dream to new investors. But you, having already experienced the return to reality that the prior managers experienced, are left holding the bag.

This is the way it works for investors who chase performance, whether on their own or at the behest of a sales rep; condemned to a life of poor returns and frustrating investment experiences.

Just say no. "No" to star ratings, "no" to hot managers, "no" to the whole Wall Street game. Choose investments based on fees, turnover and style adherence – or make sure you have an advisor who is doing the same. These are the things that *can* be controlled in the investment experience, and that is a much better way to raise your chances of enjoying great long-term performance going forward than by focusing on performance itself.

Who'd have thought?

## MYTH 3: It's All about Performance

FACT: It is one of the great ironies of investing that the more you make investment decisions based on performance, the more likely you are to experience poor performance. The reality is that the performance of stocks, funds and managers is usually attributable to what market sectors have recently been in favor. Since those sectors cycle in and out of favor quickly and unpredictably, investors who chase returns usually miss the run-up and arrive just in time for the downturn.

SOLUTION: Since you can't control which segments of the market are going to be hot going forward, select investment vehicles based on factors that you *can* control in the investment process: sales charges, expense ratios, and trading. Keeping such expenses to a minimum (or, in the case of sales charges, avoiding them altogether) is much more predictive of future success than chasing returns.

# MYTH 4

*"Much success can be attributed to inactivity. Most investors cannot resist the temptation to constantly buy and sell."*

*– Warren Buffett*

**The ancient Greek physicist** Archimedes was famous for his saying, "Give me a lever long enough, and a fulcrum on which to place it, and I can move the world."

A good paraphrase of this as it relates to investing money might be, "Give me a timeframe long enough, and a prudent strategy in which to place it, and I can make you very, very wealthy." (Granted, it's not an especially catchy paraphrase, but it accomplishes my point in this chapter so I am going with it.)

The interesting thing is that most investors will swear up-and-down that they know this already – that, over time, the market will make you wealthy. And yet most people do not get wealthy investing because they don't stay in the market long enough for that to happen. They move in and out. They jump from stock to stock, sector to sector, fund to fund. They let their emotions push them right over the cliff, often with the willing assistance of a sales rep masquerading as an advisor.

So where is the breakdown – the wrench in the process that gets between what investors know to be true (the market will make you rich over time) and what they actually *do*, which is to move around a lot and prevent the market from making them rich?

In a word, it is this: The Unknown. (Okay, *two* words.)

It is easy to sit here today and look back over the last thirty or forty years and marvel at how simple it would have been to let the market enrich you. If you had just invested $100,000 *there* (say, 1967) and patiently let it grow in an S&P 500 index fund until *there* (say, 2007) your investment would have grown to about $5,200,000. How hard is that? Any idiot could do it…right?

And what of all the turmoil the market had to overcome during that forty-year time span? All the scary things that had to be endured? Vietnam… Watergate… The Oil Crisis… The Cold War… The '87 Market Crash… The Gulf War… The Tech Bubble… Y2K… 9/11… Afghanistan… Iraq…

*Pish posh*, you say (I'm paraphrasing again), *those were all events that the market ultimately overcame, most of them with little trouble.*

So true. So now let me ask you about the future. Will you invest all your assets in the stock market today and let it sit for the next thirty years, and guarantee me you'll never once move it around during that time period?

*Well*, you say, *that's just, um…different. Because no one really knows what's going to happen going forward.*

There you have it: The disconnect. The wrench in the process. History is a linear thing, and it is difficult to think back in time and remember (or imagine) what it was like to have been an investor during a time such as the 1973-74 bear market, when the S&P 500 lost ground 23 out of 24 months, finishing 48% lower in the process. We see that event now as ancient history, a movie that might once have been scary but, since we know how it ends, we don't fear it. But we can't see the future that way. We don't know how events are going to resolve themselves, and it's that kernel of fear that keeps us from doing what seems so obvious to us in retrospect, which is to ignore the short-term noise, hang around in the market and make a lot of money.

Interestingly, however, it is this very thing – The Unknown – that earns you your money. As investors, we are rewarded for risking our capital in the stock market in the form of higher returns than bonds or cash will give us. Corporations must create enough shareholder value for investors to justify why they didn't just go buy the company's bonds. This is known as the *risk premium*. The risk premium is the return stocks deliver above what investors can obtain in so-called "risk free" government bonds. Historically that premium has been a pretty consistent 8%.

The thing is, this risk premium is not generated uniformly across the universe of stocks; obviously, some stocks generate more value than others. Nor is it delivered in a smooth, steady manner over time; there are long periods (such as the 1930s and 1970s and, for large stocks at least, the current decade) when there is a risk "penalty," so to speak, for investing in stocks – when investors would have earned *more* money in treasury bills than they did in the stock market.

This all ties directly back to The Unknown, for that is the Faustian bargain that investors have to accept when they invest in stocks. To get the premium, you have to come to terms with the fact that there are risks out there in the future that you can't know and can't quantify. And you must sit calmly with your hands folded in your lap and assume that risk if you want to make the returns that stocks historically provide.

*But I don't want to accept it,* you say.

None of us does, dear reader; none of us does. But if one wants to make stock market rates-of-return then one has no choice but to invest in the stock market.

This is all well and good on paper, but the vast majority of investors can't handle it in practice. They want all the upside and none of the downside, and so they move around in the market constantly in a futile attempt to avoid the risks that are inherent to stock investing. But, alas, all they really manage to avoid are the returns the market was trying to give them.

The reason they miss those returns is very simple. The stock market doesn't blithely distribute its gains like a child tossing rose pedals through a meadow. Instead it jam-packs massive gains into just a few trading days a year, usually when you least expect it. Miss a few of those and you are toast, as seen in the following chart:

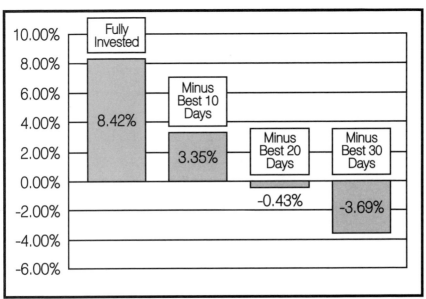

### Missing a Few Good Days Dramatically Reduces Your Returns

*S&P 500 Index: December 31,1996 – December 31, 2006*

It is a sobering thought that over a 10-year time period – somewhere around 2,520 trading days – all of the return premium that the stock market has to offer was essentially bottled up into 10 days, or .03%. Removed of those few days, stocks earned the equivalent of money-market rates of return. Lose a few more such days and you're in the red. (This is what we call a "razor-thin margin of error.")

So it is no wonder that study after study shows investors are failing miserably in their investment efforts. Most investors simply can't sit still and end up out of the market for the days that matter most.

As is true of most things in life, oftentimes those "best days" in the market come when we least expect it. Hearken back with me to March 2003. The S&P 500 is down almost 50% and counting. Enron, Arthur Andersen, WorldCom and countless dot-coms have disappeared into thin air. September 11 is still fresh in everyone's mind thanks to daily terror alerts. Our soldiers are poised to enter Iraq and encounter, we are told at the time, a madman dictator sitting on a stockpile of weapons of mass destruction the likes of which the world has never seen (oh well). And virtually every talking head on TV is predicting that the stock market will tank to levels rivaling the 1929 market crash.

For investors, it was about as depressing a scenario as it gets. So guess what happens? Stocks do exactly what everyone is least expecting. Beginning March 11, 2003, the stock market goes on a tear, shooting straight up over the next eight trading sessions, at the end of which time the S&P 500 index has gained more than 12%. Six weeks later the S&P has gained nearly 20%. By year's end, the S&P has gained 40% from its low point in March, and the Russell 2000 index of small stocks has gained 60%! Only millions of investors have missed all of the gains, sitting on the sidelines, having bailed out of the market and fled to the "safety" of cash and bond funds after panicking at some point during the preceding three-year bear market.

Here's the good news: If you are well diversified, no movement is required *even in times of market turmoil.* Sure, you will experience periodic declines in the market; sometimes there's no avoiding them. But when you spread your assets across dozens of asset classes and thousands of stocks covering markets all over the world, you are essentially making a bet on capitalism itself. Now, if you're Kim Jong Il, perhaps that doesn't really resonate with you. But for most citizens of the free world, it provides a measure of comfort, because that bet has paid off handsomely and consistently for the better part of three centuries now.

It therefore makes sense for you to invest both for breadth (across the broad stock market) as well as for length (over many years) to capture this risk premium and avoid the problems that come from investing in too few stocks and too short a period of time. Such a plan will help ensure that you will be in the market when those gaudy gains come flying around the bend just when we all least expect it.

No action required.

## MYTH 4: Activity Is Good

FACT: Investors allow fear of the unknown to coerce them into making rash decisions with their investments. Those decisions are often encouraged by "advisors" (product-compensated sales people) who convince the investor that moving around to avoid/capitalize on current market conditions is wise. In reality, activity in a portfolio is usually detrimental and causes investors to miss out on the crucial few days of huge gains the market delivers, usually when we least expect it. This constant activity is the reason investor returns trail market returns by a wide margin.

SOLUTION: The only justifiable investment activity is related to portfolio management (rebalancing, reallocating, tax-loss harvesting, etc.). Outside of this, history shows that the less you move your money around, the more you will be worth.

# MYTH 5

*"The investor's chief problem – and even his worst enemy – is likely to be himself."*

**– Benjamin Graham, "Security Analysis," 1934**

**Have you ever played** along with the game show *Jeopardy* from the comfort of your easy chair? If you're like me, you watch the show and cherry pick the answers you know, blurting them out so your spouse can hear you from the other room and be impressed with the massive body of knowledge you possess. (You especially love the sports categories, when the otherwise brainy contestants just stare blankly at the camera to questions like, "I am the world's best golfer and my name rhymes with Figer…")

When the show is done, you bask in the glow of your intellectual prowess, figuring you could be in the Tournament of Champions if you really wanted to. But, geez, who's got the time?

Here's the problem. On the show, the contestants get penalized for giving the wrong answers to questions, and their scores drop accordingly. You and I in our La-Z-Boys conveniently forget about the ones we guessed wrong and focus only on the ones we got right. We erroneously think we are doing great because we don't hold ourselves accountable for our mistakes. If we were really on that show they'd probably invoke the mercy rule and call off the game after the first round.

This is a phenomenon that translates to the investment world. Investors, as a lot, dramatically over-estimate their successes and come down with collective amnesia about their failures. They believe their efforts at do-it-yourself investing to be far more successful than they really are, when in reality their efforts cause them to miss out on investment returns that were there for the taking if they had invested properly.

Professor John R. Nofsinger of Washington State University wrote a fascinating book on this subject entitled *The Psychology of Investing*. For this book, Professor Nofsinger conducted a variety of studies among do-it-yourself investors in which he gauged their perceptions about their success against their actual investment results. He noted the impact of "cognitive dissonance" on investors — essentially, the inability of investors to mesh their belief that they had made good investment decisions with factual information pointing to the contrary:

*Investors seek to reduce psychological pain by adjusting their beliefs about the success of past investment choices. For example, at one point in time an investor will make a decision to purchase a mutual fund. Over time, performance information about the fund will either validate or put into question the wisdom of picking the mutual fund. To reduce cognitive dissonance, the investor's brain will filter out or reduce the negative information and fixate on the positive information. Therefore, investor memory of past performance is better than actual investment performance.*[11]

Professor Nofsinger pointed to a study in which investors were asked two questions about the return on their mutual-fund investments during the previous year: (1) What was the return last year? (2) By how much did you beat the market?

The researchers posed the questions to two groups of investors: architects, and members of the American Association of Individual Investors (AAII). Suffice it to say both groups are represented by highly educated individuals, and the members of the AAII have a professed interest in investing as well.

With the group comprised of architects, the researchers found that they recalled an investment performance that was on average 6.22% higher than the actual return. The architects also over-estimated the amount by which they had "beat" the market by 4.62%.[12]

Given the extraordinarily difficult task of beating the market even by a couple of percentage points, it is highly likely that most of the architects thought they were beating the market when the opposite was true.

The study also found the amateur investors from the AAII group were wearing rose-colored glasses about their returns. The group over-estimated their performance by 3.40% on average and over-estimated the percentage by which they had beat the market by 5.11%![13]

In other words (and with apologies to Garrison Keilor), all investors believe themselves to be above average.

It's easy to see how this happens. You see gains in your portfolio in strong markets and you feel like you're doing well. Your investments decline in down markets, but so did everyone else's, so you figure you're doing about the same. Sure, you've got a couple of dogs in your portfolio, but you don't focus on those. You more than made up for it with a couple of high flyers that have grown dramatically.

At the root of this problem is the fact that very few investors have the ability or inclination to track their true investment performance, net of fees and commissions, on a time-weighted basis. Such calculations are inordinately complex and require expensive software to calculate. This lack of a real, bottom-line number is a major impediment to investment success, because it allows you to make hunches and suppositions about how you are doing. And, as we saw above, the human ego being what it is, investors almost always assume they are doing better than they are. We are hard-wired to be this way, to block out pain and focus on the positive; it's what keeps the human race moving along. But this instinct is very destructive when it comes to investing because it keeps you complacent in a portfolio that is not doing as well as it should, secure in the misguided belief that you are "doing okay."

There is another, even more destructive force at work with individual investors today, an affliction that seems to permeate all aspects of life in the modern era – the unquenchable thirst for instant gratification. Rationally, investors may know that they can enrich themselves over time by being prudent and letting compounding work its miracles over time. But emotionally, who wants to wait around for that when there's free money to be made out there? We've all seen the stories about the little company that hits it big with some new product, sending its stock from $1 to $20 a share in a week. Or the hedge fund that generated the 150% return last year when the market was up only 5%. Who among us hasn't calculated the value of a $10,000 investment in such a thing and marveled at all the money we could have made *if only we'd been in on the ground floor?*

This is akin to beating yourself over the head because you didn't pick the winning numbers in Powerball last Friday; the odds of success are about the same, as is your ability to go back in time and do anything about it. And yet this pipedream plagues individual investors, sending them off on a never-ending, fruitless quest for easy money.

Here's a vivid example: Beginning in the summer of 2005 foreign stocks went on a tear, posting significantly higher gains than U.S. stocks, a trend that continued through 2006. At that point a cautious person might have realized that it would be extremely risky behavior to overload in foreign stocks in hopes of riding the performance wave, as all waves crash eventually. Apparently, though, such thinking escaped the investing public: According to the Investment Company Institute, individual investors put $81.28 billion into foreign funds through the first half of 2007, compared with just $8.09 billion into broad-based U.S. stock mutual funds. That means more than 90% of mutual fund inflows from U.S. investors went into foreign funds!

Let me be the first to say that foreign stocks are an important part of a well-diversified portfolio. But, clearly, all those millions of investors putting all those billions of dollars in foreign funds weren't thinking about prudent diversification; *they wanted in on some of that action!* (Predictably, foreign stocks tanked even more than U.S. stocks during the market volatility that began in July 2007 and accelerated in 2008.)

If you think this is anecdotal evidence, here's a pop quiz for you. Just fill in the blanks with your best guess before you check the answers that follow:

1.  Today the average holding period for a mutual fund is _____.

2.  Today the average holding period for an individual stock is _____.

Answer 1: Just over three years.[14]
Answer 2: About 10 months.[15]

Do you realize that this is ABSOLUTE INSANITY? People are not only not investing for the long-term, they're not even investing for the *mid term.* (Heck, it's hard to even call 10 months "short term"; I propose we go with *micro term.*)

It gets worse. In recent years the brokerage industry has been touting complex investments such as commodities, derivatives and options to individual investors as a way to magically hedge away their stock-market risk "just like the pros." Implicit in this sales pitch is the notion that there are ways around the risk/reward equilibrium *if you are smart enough*. We saw how well this worked out for those who tried to pretend that mortgage-backed derivatives were somehow less risky than the mortgage holders behind them.

There is no, I repeat NO, way around the risk/reward equilibrium. Risk and reward go hand-in-hand. It is possible to diversify away unnecessary risk, but it is not possible to just "hedge away" all of the risk that comes from stock investing by counter-balancing your portfolio with exotic and volatile products such as derivatives and commodities. As we saw in ample evidence in the fall of 2008, there is simply no telling how such products will react in every market environment.

All of this fruitless activity on the part of individual investors – chasing returns, dabbling with exotic investments, bailing out of the market in a downturn – results in dramatic underperformance. Sadly, most investors have no idea how poorly they are really faring, because they don't have an accurate understanding of their true investment returns and turn a blind eye toward the pain.

Feel the pain. Look at your investable assets and ask yourself if it's enough – or will be enough at your current rate – to sustain you through a quarter century of retirement. If the answer makes you squirm, then it's time to sit yourself down, have a little heart-to-heart chat, and get serious about investing the right way.

## MYTH 5: Investors Do All Right for Themselves

FACT: Do-it-yourself investors are plagued by "cognitive dissonance" – the brain's tendency to focus on the positive and block out the negative, which leads investors to bask in their successes and conveniently ignore their disasters. Investors also suffer from the modern malady that is the desire for instant gratification, churning their accounts in a fruitless quest for easy money. As a result, individual investor performance tends to be much worse than what those investors realize, because investors don't adequately track the costs of trading and taxes. This lack of a true "net" performance number keeps them from having to face the consequences of their actions.

SOLUTION: If you are inclined to manage your own money, make sure you have a disciplined plan and follow it religiously, never allowing short-term flights of fancy to divert you from your goals. Use investment software to help you calculate your true net performance so that you have an accurate sense of what kind of returns you are really generating, on a net basis, in your portfolio. If all of that sounds like too much work, find an independent, fee-only advisor who will do all of that for you.

# MYTH 6

## The Media Is a Good Source of Investment Advice

*"If you want the truth, it's going to cost you more than a quarter."*
*– Lewis Grizzard*
**Southern humorist and newspaper columnist, (1946-1994)**

**Time for a dirty** little secret.

I was not a finance major in college. I wasn't even a business major.

I was, in truth, a *journalism* major. (*Gasp!*)

In fact, not only was I a journalism major, but I was actually employed in the field for a short time after college, working first as a reporter for a suburban daily newspaper outside of Atlanta, then as a magazine editor. In the scant two years I was in journalism, I learned a valuable life lesson, as all dewy-eyed college graduates inevitably must: the simple joys of food, shelter, clothing and transportation should not be underestimated. And making $15,000 a year was not going to provide for much of any of those things.

41

Thus was my foray into journalism a short one. Nonetheless, it was quite useful for me to learn the tricks of the trade. And the primary trick of the journalism trade is this: It doesn't matter how well you understand your subject, only that you can report on it intelligently for a thousand or so words in a manner that will interest people. It doesn't even matter if your premise is *correct*. It only matters that you can find people to substantiate your angle.

Oftentimes I would find myself expounding upon the virtues of, say, a school redistricting plan. As a twenty-three-year-old single male, I really had no knowledge of, much less interest in, school redistricting. But I had a job to do, and in the course of three or four conversations with people well-versed in the subject, I would be able to deduce the salient points relating to school redistricting and write an article on the topic that made it sound as if I actually had a clue, which I most assuredly did not.

Journalists are masters of fakery, albeit in an honorable sort of way. They are canny people who can quickly glean the relevant facts about a subject that they first learned about only a few minutes prior and regurgitate it in a reasonably coherent manner. At a Christmas party a few years ago I had a brief conversation with a newspaper editor, and I thought he put it best: Journalists, he said, are a mile wide and an inch deep.

Never was this more true than with investing. With a few notable exceptions, reporters who cover investing typically fall under the sway of the Wall Street hype machine and come to believe that investing is exciting and dramatic.

In truth, the principles of investment success are really quite boring. Diversify effectively. Control costs and taxes. Control your emotions. Be patient. (*Yawn.*) Of course, as we have noted, while these principles are simple enough to grasp, they are quite difficult to employ, as emotions get the better of nearly all investors sooner or later. But the fact remains that this "secret" to investment success is there for all to see, and can be communicated in a few short paragraphs.

This leaves reporters in a bind, at least the ones who understand it, because how many different ways can you write that story? Imagine walking into the grocery store and seeing the cover of Money Magazine with its giant typeface headlines screaming:

"AGAIN THIS MONTH WE REVIEW THE FOUR PRINCIPLES OF INVESTMENT SUCCESS!" You pick up the magazine and find it is only a single page, with the principles explained on the back cover. And that's the whole magazine. End of story.

How many times are you going to buy *that* magazine?

Obviously, not very often, which gets to the root of the dilemma: You simply can't move magazines (or draw viewers) telling that story day in and day out. And, shocking as this may be, *moving magazines – not delivering sound investment advice – is what those companies are in business to do.*

The result is that, even for reporters who know better, the pressure to slant one's coverage to the sensational (e.g. hot funds, hot managers, hot stocks) is insurmountable, because that is what is exciting and that is what readers want to believe and that, therefore, is what sells. Syndicated columnist Jane Bryant Quinn calls it "Investment Pornography," and she's right. It is prurient material, designed to titillate the reader into buying it off the shelf. The fact that it's really, really bad advice is beside the point.

If you think I'm being harsh I offer the following as exhibit A: In 1999, *Fortune* published a telling column from one of its reporters, who had come to the magazine from one of the tabloid-like investment publications that are always touting the "Five Funds You Must Own Now!" So ashamed was this reporter of her sordid past that she published the column anonymously. Given the nature of her confession, one can hardly blame her:

*Mutual funds reporters lead a secret investing life. By day we write "Six Funds to Buy NOW!" We seem to delight in dangerous sectors like technology. We appear fascinated with one-week returns. By night, however, we invest in sensible index funds.*

*I know, because I once was one of those reporters – condemned to write a new fund story every day – when I covered funds for an online publication. I was ignorant. My only personal experience had been bumbling into a load fund until a colleague steered me to an S&P 500 index fund. I worried I'd misdirect readers, but I was assured that in personal-finance journalism it doesn't matter if the advice turns out to be right, as long as it's logical. You're supposed to produce the most stories "that end in investment decisions," so publications substitute formulas for wisdom. The formula for recommending funds: Filter according to returns, then add something trendy – high tech, no tech, whatever. For an extra twist, omit funds with loads or new managers.*

*The problem is that recent returns, whether from one week or the old standby three years, don't predict future results. Nothing predicts future results. The best you can do is to hold on to low-cost, diversified funds and be oblivious to short-term static.*

*Unfortunately, rational, pro-index-fund stories don't sell magazines, cause hits on Websites, or boost Nielsen ratings. So rest assured: You'll keep on seeing those enticing but worthless "Six Funds to Buy NOW!" headlines as long as there are personal-finance media.*[16]

There you have it, straight from the source. And though this reporter learned a lot by the time she wrote this article, she admits she was ignorant when she was writing all those hot fund stories. This is typical of most, though not all, media when it comes to covering investments. The reporter may have been moved there from sports, or obits, or the lifestyle section, and often the stay on the business desk writing investment stories is no more than a year or two. So there is no time and little interest in really becoming expert at what makes for successful investing.

As a result, reporters typically fall under the spell of the brokerage analysts such as those we see on the cable networks a dozen times a day, who want people to believe that investing is all about movement. The analysts are smart, slick, highly compensated individuals, and they certainly sound like they know what they are talking about. And so neophyte reporters are all too happy to open their mouths and accept the spoon-fed pabulum that these analysts want them to believe. Even those reporters who do make a career out of the investment industry usually gain their world view from this, the sales side of the business, so though they become more familiar with the workings and terminology of the industry, they still don't *get* it.

These are the twin forces of wealth destruction in America, Wall Street and the media, the former witting and the latter, for the most part, unwitting. They feed on each other, the media desperate for content and sensationalism and Wall Street always standing at the ready to deliver for them. At the other end of the portal sits the lonely viewer, clinging to his nest egg like a child holding his security blanket, sure that Mr. Analyst must know what he's talking about. After all, when's the last time you remember an analyst appearing on a news show being called on the carpet for being wrong? It doesn't happen. So there is no disincentive for analysts to get on TV and make whatever ridiculous assertions they want to make, because there is no accountability. In fact, the more outlandish the prediction, the greater the likelihood of getting some face time on the cable networks. The networks welcome them with open arms because of their insatiable need for sensationalistic content.

Some of the biggest offenders in this category are the financial news websites, such as those operated by CNN, Fox, MSN, etc. In fairness, it must be daunting for those who are in charge of these sites to have to churn out so much copy every day, only to find that half of what they've written is obsolete by noon (*"Stocks sell off on higher oil prices!"* *oops…um…hold on… "Stocks shrug off higher oil prices, make big gains!"* *wait…dang… "Stocks in volatile trading as oil prices fluctuate!" Wait…strike that…)*

As with the prior example from *Fortune* magazine, all of this pressure to produce copy (and not just any copy, but copy that makes people want to hang around your web site) lends added pressure to the writers to come up with sensational angles that can be quickly explored and will grab the Internet surfer who just happens by the page.

In August of 2003 I came across a story on the CNN/Money website that speaks to this. The headline of the article was "The Guns of August," with the sub-headline below reading "It's not hard to find excuses to get out of the market right now" – dire words that would stop any innocent surfer in his tracks. The premise of the article was that, historically, August is a bad month for stocks, and the period from August to October is a gauntlet that no investor wants to run:

*It looks as if stocks have fallen into their typical seasonal pattern, with a big jump out of a messy October that peters out into sleepy, rangebound trading once summer gets underway. That's troubling, because seasonally August and September have historically been awful months for the market.*

*It's easy to come up with reasons to sell stocks now, and even easier to come up with reasons not to buy any more ... [It] seems like there are good chances seasonal effects could kick in, because fundamental investors are being given such good excuses to get out.*[17]

In other words: Don't be an idiot – get out of the market now. To the reporter, this sounds like a perfectly logical premise. It is historically verifiable and there are smart people who know the business who will go on record agreeing with you.

The problem is that it's not *true*. Or, more accurately, it's true when it's true and it isn't when it isn't. It is true that, most of the time, the late summer/early fall months have been rough ones for stocks. If you look back at the 50 years from 1957 through 2006, stocks declined 29 times during the three-month period from August through October. But that leaves us with 21 times when stocks enjoyed gains during that three-month span. When these time periods will be bad and when they won't is purely a guessing game, despite what the reporter wants to believe. And it leaves out the hardest part of market timing, which is when to get *back in* the market.

In this case, the unfortunate reader who followed this well-meaning reporter's advice did not fare well. From the date of publication of that article through year-end 2003, the S&P 500 index gained 13%, while the Russell 2000 index of small stocks gained 24%. Those are returns that an investor who followed the reporter's advice never got back – a very real opportunity cost that cost the investor very real money.

This "movement is good" mindset becomes especially prevalent in the media during times of market turmoil. Back in the late summer of 1998, the world's stock markets plunged dramatically in just a few days' time when a foreign currency crisis roiled the markets. The downturn was triggered by a combination of unsettling events in Asia and Russia, none of which matter now (further to my point) but suffice it to say the dial of market emotions was set to "fear."

On the worst of these days, when the S&P 500 dropped about 7% in a single trading session, I got a call from a reporter for *The Wall Street Journal* who was looking for the view from the front, so to speak. What was I saying to my clients who were calling? How was I handling the Herculean task of keeping them calm in the midst of this market panic? What moves were we making in our clients' portfolios in response to this market plunge?

I wasn't doing anything, I told him. There were no calls. There was no panic. There were no moves. All was well, at my firm at least.

Total silence. Somewhere a cricket chirped.

"You mean to tell me that you haven't gotten a *single call* from a client today?" the reporter pressed me. There was a tone of dubious incredulity in his voice, which is to say he thought I was B.S.-ing him.

I told him, truthfully, that we had not. I told him we had worked with our clients to explain the realities of investing in the market. (To review:

Short term, stocks go up and down. Long term, stocks go up.) We had also worked hard on the front end to be sure they were invested in a strategy they could live with in good *and* bad markets, so that when times like this arrived, our clients were well within their comfort range and no movement was requested or required.

"Thanks," he said, and then, in that affectionate manner New York reporters have about them, he hung up on me. I could almost hear the words DO NOT CALL being typed next to my name in the *Journal's* source database. I knew I would not be invited to play in their reindeer games anymore. (Ten years and no calls later, it appears I was right.)

When I read the article the next day, I could see why he was miffed with me. All the traders and brokers interviewed in the story were talking about what a crazy day it had been, how they had been busy moving their clients out of the market and "onto the sidelines." The angle of the article was all about the movement that was going on in the face of the market turmoil. Notably absent were any quotes from the dipwad, Pollyanna advisor in Atlanta who insisted everything was fine.

Were I to track the reporter down today I'm sure he would have absolutely no interest in the fact that the intervening years have proven me right. He wasn't writing a story about successful investing; he was writing a story about *the action*. And that's what his focus is on today, too.

There's nothing morally wrong with writing about the action per se. It's just that so many investors who read these articles come to the mistaken conclusion that this is what successful investing is all about. *It's not*. It's what trading is all about. It's what speculating is all about. But it's got nothing to do with long-term investment success.

Certainly there are some writers who are exceptions to this rule, such as Scott Burns of the *Dallas Morning News*, Jason Zweig and Brett Arends of *The Wall Street Journal*, John Wasik of *Bloomberg.com* and Walter Updegrave of *Money* magazine, five writers who have a fine grasp of the fundamentals of investment success and a healthy skepticism of the Wall Street hype machine. We would commend their writings to anyone.

There are others, no doubt, but the fact that only five writers come quickly to mind is further evidence of the original premise of this chapter:

*Don't take investment advice from the media.*

## MYTH 6: The Media Is a Good Source of Investment Advice

FACT: The media does not exist to provide you sound investment advice (nor is it obligated to). The media is in business to turn a profit, and that profit is made by drawing readers, viewers, or web visitors to their content and keeping them there as long as possible. *This is only possible when the content is dramatic, and the principles of prudent investing are decidedly not dramatic.* Wall Street is expert at feeding the media with the type of sensational content that hooks investors by appealing either to their fear or greed as dictated by the current market environment, thereby furthering its endless need to have individual investors in a constant state of buying and selling.

SOLUTION: In the vast sea of talking heads in the media who do little more than make things worse for investors, there are a few lonely voices who continually preach the same righteous investment gospel we have espoused in this book. Turn to these sages to reaffirm that you are doing the right thing, and let the rest of the chatter fade away like the white noise that it is.

# MYTH 7

## Invest in Good Companies

*"I wouldn't even think about selling my stock. You don't get off a winning horse. My horse dropped dead on me. "*

*— Enron employee, age 63,*
*who had 100% of his retirement assets invested in company stock*[18]

**I remember my grandfather's** investment portfolio.

It was very typical of an investor in Atlanta in his day, comprised entirely of four stocks: Trust Company of Georgia (now SunTrust), Coca-Cola, Delta and Genuine Parts. He amassed his positions in those stocks over the better part of fifty years. He believed in those companies, knew many of their executives from church and social clubs, understood what they did and how they did it. He was loyal to them, never selling his positions in a bad market, and in return the stocks were good to him.

During the middle part of the twentieth century – between roughly the Great Depression and the market crash of October 1987 – this was a perfectly reasonable approach to investing. Information moved much slower than today, trading volume in the market was modest, and you had a sense of comfort and control about the stocks you owned. If you began to grow concerned that one of your companies was off track – say you played golf with the CEO and he spent most of his time sipping on a flask and talking about his Swiss bank account – you had plenty of time to sidestep a potential disaster. You'd unwind your position in an orderly fashion and invest in another company you knew well and were fond of.

For the most part, if you were disciplined in your behavior, you could feel pretty well assured that buying the stocks of a few good companies would create great wealth for you over time with relatively little downside. Sort of like a Super Treasury Bill.

This ain't my – or your – grandfather's stock market anymore.

In many ways, the events of Monday, October 19, 1987, signaled the end of those simpler times for investors. On that day, the S&P 500 stock index declined 22% in a single trading session. Many individual stocks declined by half or more. Most troubling was that there was no single event to which the panic selloff could be attributed. While the selling initially began in overseas markets that day, it was greatly compounded by program trading in the United States, in which institutional investors had programmed their computers to automatically sell huge blocks of stock if prices dropped below certain levels. When those program trades kicked in, they began to trigger *other* program trades, and in short order a tidal wave of selling cascaded through the world's capital markets.

While the S&P 500 recovered its losses in less than two years, Black Monday, as it came to be known, was a wake-up call for investors. Technology had ushered in a new era, one in which the twin emotions of investing – fear and greed – could be introduced into the daily workings of the stock market like never before. Pandora's Box had been opened; now, computers and the free flow of information both enabled and caused massive amounts of stocks to be traded on a daily basis.

Over the next decade, the business environment for publicly traded companies morphed from competitive to brutal. Analysts and shareholders became obsessed with enhancing stock price above all else and exhibited little patience for companies – and their executives – who weren't obsessed with the same. CEOs came to be viewed as the business equivalent of NFL head coaches: Just win, baby. Or you're gone.

Today, nostalgia and loyalty no longer have a place in the global economy. Companies that miss their earnings targets can expect significant, instantaneous declines in their stock prices, and any hint of long-term problems can sink the price of a stock by half or more in very short order as investors head for the exits.

In short, running a publicly traded company in today's market environment is as much about surviving as it is about thriving, and the super blue chips such as those my grandfather took shelter in all those years are no more immune to this than small, start-up companies. Here's a vivid example: On March 7, 2000, consumer products giant Procter & Gamble announced that its earnings would fall short of analysts' expectations. By the end of the day, P&G's stock had fallen from $88 to $55 a share – a 40% decline in a single session, for one of the world's largest and most revered companies. All told the stock declined 55% in just six weeks' time.

This was a short-term situation for Procter & Gamble, whose stock price has recovered nicely in recent years. But I bet it didn't feel short term for all those retirees who had a huge chunk of their nest egg in P&G stock. Imagine if you had $500,000 in your retirement account and then the next day you had $300,000. And here you thought you were being prudent by investing in a big, well-known company. It is scenarios such as these that plague today's investors in individual stocks, causing them to wake up at 3 a.m. in a cold sweat with this burning question screaming in their brain:

*Can IBM meet its earnings target on Tuesday???*

That may sound ridiculous, but I would wager that if most of your assets were concentrated in IBM, you'd think it was pretty rational. This is a fairly recent development for investors; my grandfather and his compadres always paid close attention to the stocks they owned, watching the tickers, following earnings, etc., and they undoubtedly had some time periods when they had to muster their intestinal fortitude and stay the course despite unsettling events in the market. But they never had that white-knuckles-on-the-dashboard kind of feeling that afflicts today's owners of individual stocks, who must always wonder if there is some *thing* out there – an accounting fraud, an earnings restatement, a product-liability lawsuit – that will put the company under in short order. In today's volatile stock market, there is a great deal more dispersion between strong performers and poor performers than there was 30 or 40 years ago. As a result, the potential to experience devastating losses in an individual stock – even a big, blue-chip stock – is much greater than in generations past.

This is a difficult pill for many investors to swallow, especially those whose families have owned large positions of low cost-basis stock for generations. We often struggle with such investors to convince them of the wisdom of liquidating their concentrated stock positions and paying taxes to boot. Many a baby boomer is consumed with guilt at such a thought, remembering all the years their parents dutifully held onto their blue chips in good times and bad, amassing comfortable nest eggs thanks to their disciplined behavior. The thought of selling those stocks and paying taxes to boot feels downright treasonous.

As an investment advisor in Atlanta in the 1990s, I faced this challenge on what seemed like a daily basis with investors who held large positions of stock in the Coca-Cola Company. If you look up "sacred cow" in an Atlanta dictionary, you'll see a picture of a Coke bottle. Coke built Atlanta. It put the city on the map. It made a lot of people in these parts very, very wealthy. It is the world's most iconic brand, so imagine what that means in its hometown. It runs through people's veins here. In Atlanta, if someone asks you for a Coke and you give them a Pepsi instead…well, let's just say you might as well slap them across the face with a glove and challenge them to a duel.

On top of this, Coke was enjoying a period of time, during the 1980s and '90s, in which it was *the* most profitable blue-chip stock in the world. Its head honcho, Roberto Goizueta, was one of the original Superstar CEOs, a brilliant Svengali who guided the soft-drink giant through a maze of difficult market conditions and onto a path of, what seemed, never-ending prosperity. By 1997, Mr. Goizueta had generated more wealth for Coke investors than any CEO in history with a total return on Coke stock of more than 7,100 percent. That meant a $100,000 investment in Coke in 1981 – something quite a few Atlantans possessed – would have been worth around $7,100,000 by 1997, including reinvested dividends.

Imagine, then, the reaction when I told people in those days that they had a great deal of risk being concentrated in a single stock – even if it was Coke – and that they should consider paying the taxes and diversifying. The suggestion that investors concentrated in this stock should diversify to avoid heretofore unrealized risks required a certain amount of, shall we say, chutzpah. I often thought about wearing full body armor into a meeting where I was going to propose such a thing. The look of sheer horror on people's faces was memorable.

*Diversify? Daddy's Coke stock? Are you mad???*

It seemed quite mad, no doubt. But then something unexpected happened: In September 1997, Mr. Goizueta was diagnosed with advanced lung cancer. Six weeks later he was dead. Just like that, the man many considered to be the world's best CEO was gone, and the void at the top of the Coca-Cola tower on North Avenue in downtown Atlanta was palpable. Having had only four CEOs in its first century of existence, Coke shuffled three different people through the position in the next ten years. A variety of problems — from product safety to product development to relations with its bottlers — dragged on the company. What once seemed like an unstoppable head of steam for Coke evaporated into thin air.

Over the next seven years, from January 1, 1998, through December 31, 2005, Coke stock experienced a cumulative decline of 31%. Over the same period of time, the S&P 500 index gained 45%.

For those few Coke investors who had many millions of dollars, the losses were sustainable, if not necessarily enjoyable. But for most Coke shareholders — including many heirs who had received an after-tax, divided slice of their family's original, large stake — the loss was devastating. Such investors could scarcely afford to lose almost a third of their net worth and a significant amount of time that their assets could have — and should have — been growing had they diversified. I still recall speaking with a potential client of our firm in 1998 who told me of his plans to liquidate his concentrated position in Coke stock once it got back to $80 a share. Ten years later, he's still waiting.

In some ways, though, Coke investors got lucky, for in these parts there is a whole other group of investors who lost everything: the shareholders of Delta Air Lines. Like many of its airline cousins, Delta succumbed in 2006 to Chapter 11 bankruptcy, rendering its stock worthless. I imagine that its investors, if given the chance, would gladly turn the clock back to 2000, sell their positions, pay the 20% capital gains tax and diversify themselves silly. Such a scenario would have been unthinkable for Delta a mere decade earlier, with oil prices around $25 a barrel and terrorism something that only happened in other countries. Who would have thought market conditions could turn so quickly against such a venerable titan and run it into the ground?

Certainly not the media. As we examined in Myth #6, when it comes to investing, the media is in love with the rearview mirror. Reporters are forever searching for a hook, and the day's hottest companies always make easy fodder for a story.

Consider *Fortune* magazine's annual list of "Most Admired Companies", a ranking compiled from the votes of thousands of business executives across the country and published with much fanfare. I have no problem with the notion of such a list; it is certainly interesting to see who the business community considers to be the best of the best. My problem comes when, as happens all too often, the reporter extrapolates that business success into an investment recommendation.

For example, looking back at that same list a decade earlier, here were *Fortune's* Most Admired Companies of 1998:

1. General Electric
2. Coca-Cola
3. Microsoft
4. Intel
5. Hewlett Packard
6. Southwest Airlines
7. Berkshire Hathaway
8. Disney
9. Johnson & Johnson
10. Merck

And here is an excerpt from the valentine, er, article in *Fortune* that accompanied that list:

*Never fall in love with a stock, investment advisers say. It's wise counsel, but you could be forgiven for ignoring it if the objects of your affection were the stocks of the ten most admired corporations in America. If you'd had the foresight to invest in these ten companies … you'd have a thoroughly diversified portfolio. You'd have* *transportation and financial services and consumer goods and capital goods and health care and information technology and entertainment, among other things. You'd own companies that make sugar water and shoes, sitcoms and spreadsheets, movies, medicines, and microchips, hardware and soft soaps, candy and dental floss. In their variety, America's ten most admired companies resemble the economy. But as they stand above the rest of corporate America in reputation, so do they tower over it in performance. If ten years ago you had bought $10,000 worth of Standard & Poor's 500 and reinvested your dividends, your estimable 17.92% annual rate of return would have compounded into $51,964 today. If you had, however, put $1,000 into each of this year's ten most admired companies, you would be sitting nearly three times prettier, with a portfolio worth $146,419.*[19]

In case you are wondering, the return for the portfolio of Most Admired Companies was 30.87% per year leading up to that article, which was published in the spring of 1998. Given that astronomical rate of return and the warm, glowy feelings of owning the day's biggest and best companies, who wouldn't have been tempted to just buy those ten stocks and kick back while you watched your money double every 2.5 years or so?

Only it didn't work out that way. Here's a look at the annual returns of those ten companies over the next decade (May 1998 through May 2008; dividends reinvested):

1. Johnson & Johnson      8.72%
2. Hewlett Packard        8.08%
3. Berkshire Hathaway     6.71%
4. Southwest Airlines     5.27%
5. Microsoft              4.65%
6. Intel                  3.52%
7. General Electric       3.26%
8. Disney                -0.08%
9. Merck                 -0.67%
10. Coca-Cola            -1.25%

Of that group, three stocks generated negative annual returns, and two more generated returns roughly in line with money-market returns. Only the top two (J&J and HP) enjoyed returns that were close to the historical long-term return of the stock market. An equally-weighted portfolio of those stocks would have generated only 4.31% annually over the next decade, not exactly the gaudy double-digit gains the reader of that article was signing up for.

It is particularly telling that the author of the story considered this group of stocks to be a "fully diversified portfolio." His logic was that the companies made a wide variety of things, so grouping them together must therefore give one good diversification. But the author lacked an understanding of diversification from an investment perspective: Owning only ten stocks, no matter how different they may be, is not adequate diversification at all, because you have significant risk related to the fates of those individual companies unrelated to the overall stock market. For example, in the bottom three from the group you had the untimely death of a superstar CEO (Roberto Goizueta of Coke), a rash of product failures and liability lawsuits (Merck) and a powerful, dynamic CEO who lost his magic touch and was ousted by shareholders (Michael Eisner of Disney). None of those things were related to the fate of the overall stock market, and all of those things cost investors in those stocks a lot of money.

This is the state of affairs we find ourselves in today: No matter how great a company has performed, no matter how many times the CEO has been featured on the cover of Forbes, no matter what your broker buddy tells you about the limitless upside of that stock, it's not worth it. It's not worth the potential disaster you could experience if you happen to be in the wrong stock. In short, it's not about the upside – it's about the *downside*. As investors in WorldCom and Delta and Pets.com and myriad other companies can attest, sometimes things don't work out fine over time. Sometimes a buy-and-hold investor can buy-and-hold that stock right into oblivion.

The good news is that this is a situation easily remedied. Investors whose assets are well diversified need not lose sleep over the fate of an individual stock, because they have exposure to thousands of securities in asset classes all over the world. Let us resolve, therefore, that while being a stock investor is a good thing, being concentrated in individual stocks is not such a good thing. A key distinction in the Darwinian world that is today's stock market.

## MYTH 7: Invest in Good Companies

FACT: For much of the 20th century, it was a perfectly prudent approach to invest your money in the stocks of a few good companies and leave your money to grow over time. But today's market is a much more volatile environment for individual stocks; good companies can experience sudden, unforeseen problems that can tank their stock price by half or more in a just a few weeks.

SOLUTION: You must diversify away the risk that comes from holding individual stocks. In today's market environment, it's not about the upside – it's about the *downside*. The potential for investors concentrated in only a few stocks to lose half or more of their portfolio value in short order is simply not worth the risk.

# MYTH 8

## Investing Is Exciting

*"The two things in life you want to be boring are your health and your investments."*

*– Unknown*

**Sorry to break it** to you: Investing is boring.

At least, *successful* investing is boring. Bad investing is very exciting, in much the same way splitting tens at the blackjack table is exciting. Your palms sweat, your heart races, and you wait in breathless anticipation while the dealer (market) turns over the cards that determine whether or not you will get away with your boneheaded decision.

Most investors struggle with investing because they fail to grasp the key difference between *speculating* and *investing*. Speculating is often assumed to be the province of aggressive traders looking to make a fortune in a hurry and with no aversion to risk. In actuality, though, the speculating mentality is broader and more subtle than that. If you have all of your assets concentrated in just a few stocks, you are essentially speculating on the fate of those companies in the future. As we noted in the previous chapter, your success will have relatively little to do with the success of the stock market – you are betting on the companies themselves. Likewise, if you are overloaded in a few sectors such as health care, energy, etc., then you are speculating that those sectors will outperform the broad stock market going forward.

Speculating can sometimes be very gratifying. Let's say your neighbor is an executive with a small, publicly traded company and she tells you they're going to do great things going forward (nothing non-public, of course). So you scrape up $10,000 and buy the stock on her encouragement and – *shazam!* – six months later you've doubled your money. You can't do that in the broad market, that's for sure!

Here's the problem: Just like a compulsive gambler, once an investor hits it big with a stock pick, it's almost impossible to walk away. You've got the fever. You start to envision how much you would be worth now if you had only invested *more*. So now you take $50,000 you've got set aside for your income taxes in April and instead plow it into additional shares of your secret stock, assuring yourself all the while that it's just seed money, that you'll have all that and a whole lot more when your taxes are due. Except the company misses its earnings forecast. The stock drops 50% in a month. Now, even though you had gained 100% originally, you're deep in the red. A few weeks later the phone rings. It's Uncle Sam. He wants his money.

This isn't far-fetched – it's a true story from one of my college friends. He learned the hard way about the dangers of confusing speculating with investing.

"But I would never do that!" you say. And it's true that most people wouldn't be so brazen as to take money set aside to pay taxes and throw it into a risky stock. On the other hand, it is a slim minority of folks who bring their brokerage statements for me to analyze that don't have some obscure tech stock sitting on their balance sheet with a $90 cost basis and a 10-cent market value. The plain fact is that when markets get hot, investors get excited, and rash decisions follow.

The "investing is exciting" mindset often leads to extreme amounts of volatility. And there is something very important you need to know about volatility:

*Volatility Bad!!!*

Stock investors have to learn to live with a certain amount of volatility, but investors take on unnecessary volatility when they embrace the notion that investing is fun and exciting. It leads them to make speculative, emotional decisions with their money, and that is the surest path to investment failure.

This speculative approach to investing is often accompanied by a lack of understanding, or at least recognition, of the exponential nature of losses. Here's an illustration: If you have a dollar, and you lose 50% of it, you are left, obviously, with 50 cents. Now, if you gain that 50% back, you are gaining it on only the remaining 50 cents, which earns you a shiny quarter, leaving you with a total of only 75 cents on the round trip. You would actually need to gain *100%* on your money to recover the original 50% drop.

Here's a real-life example of the caustic effects of volatility. For the four-year period ending December 31, 2006, the Nasdaq index enjoyed a cumulative return of more than 75%. Yet despite those gaudy gains, the Nasdaq was still *down* 40% for the seven-year period ending December 31, 2006, owing to the fact that the index declined nearly 80% from March 2000 to October 2002. Investors who hopped aboard the tech stock train in 2000 still have a very long way to go to recoup their losses.

The danger of excess volatility may seem like common sense to you, but it is a reality that escapes a great many investors. Following is a chart showing several different levels of loss, the gain needed to recoup the loss, and the number of years it would take to earn it if you gained a flat 10% rate of return every year going forward:

| Percentage Decline | Gain Needed to Get Back to Break-Even | # of Years Required* |
|---|---|---|
| 10% | 11% | 1.10 |
| 30% | 42% | 3.74 |
| 50% | 100% | 7.27 |
| 70% | 233% | 12.63 |
| 90% | 900% | 24.15 |

*A gain of 10% per year was assumed for illustrative purposes.*

Investors often do not pay enough attention to reducing volatility in their portfolio. They may bump merrily along for many years without being aware of how much volatility they could potentially experience. And then – bam! – they hit a period of time like 2000-02, and suddenly they find themselves with big losses.

That was a traumatic time for many investors. I met with dozens of prospective clients during 2001 and 2002, most of whom had been at a brokerage firm where, they learned too late, a broker had crammed their portfolio full of growth stocks. When growth stocks blew up, their portfolio blew up with it.

During the initial phase of that long market decline – between March 2000 and September 2001 – I met with many investors whose portfolios had declined around 30%. Many were reluctant to make a change, having heard the "don't sell out during a market downturn" mantra many times. But, as we have learned, you should only adopt the "buy-and-hold" mentality if you are in a well-diversified portfolio. These investors were usually not even in a "portfolio" in the true sense of the word – just a conglomeration of stocks, funds and/or annuities that the broker had sold them over the years. I urged such investors to get out of their holdings and into a prudent strategy before they found themselves in a much deeper hole. Whether they used our firm or another, I told them, they needed to get out of their product hodge-podge and into a sound strategy.

Some of those folks listened to my pleadings, but many did not, paralyzed at the thought of "locking in" a 30% loss. And then…9/11. Anthrax. Afghanistan. WorldCom. Terror alerts. Iraq. Anxiety and malaise swept the markets from mid-2001 to early 2003. Those unfortunate investors who stayed with their growth-heavy portfolios found themselves by this time with losses in the 50% to 70% range, increasing the gains they would need to recover their losses somewhere between three- and five-fold over what they would have needed down 30%. Those investors who were in retirement and drawing on their money were in especially dire straits, because now they were drawing down a much greater percentage of their nest egg, increasing the gains they would need to make *even more*.

This is how the death spiral begins. You suffer a big loss, you need to be more aggressive to make the money back. But you lose more. Now you need to be even more aggressive. Pretty soon you find yourself with 1/10th of what you had, sitting on the sidelines in CDs trying to save that last measly portion, wondering how you got into this predicament so fast. It sounds a lot like compulsive gambling, doesn't it?

The difference is that most investors don't choose to gamble this way – they either don't understand that that is what they're doing, or, more often, they put their trust in someone who is just a product salesman masquerading as an advisor. That's not a hypothetical; it happened to thousands of investors, and they still haven't recovered their standard of living.

There is another way – the way of the true investor. Like a Shogun warrior, the true investor keeps his eyes focused on the goal and steels himself to the inevitable challenges and temptations that lie in his path. The true investor knows the simple miracle of compound interest will take care of him over time, if he is patient and resourceful and resolute.

The true investor wants access to all that the stock market has to offer in terms of its much higher long-term return than bonds and cash, but there is an aversion – yea, verily, an *abhorrence!* – to taking on unnecessary risk. Instead, the true investor (or his advisor) sets about constructing the portfolio in such an efficient manner that the investor can expect to obtain the returns he needs and still remain invested in markets both good and bad.

Does that mean we never do *anything?* That we invest in a strategy and forget about it for 30 years? Absolutely not. Think of it as a house. You have kids, you expand your house. Your kids grow up and move out, you remodel your house. Your mother moves in, you build a home theater (for yourself – you'll need some place you can spend a lot of time).

But at no time are you bringing in a wrecking ball for your house. And, if a bad storm comes up, you don't flee your house for some other mythical place of "safety." Your house *is* your safe place. It's well constructed and built to stand the test of time. (Unless you live in a trailer, in which case you would definitely want to get out and go to a safer place.) (This is a good analogy for those day traders.) It's all about maintaining it and tending to it and keeping it set up so that it best suits your needs.

Likewise the true investor wants to tend to his portfolio over time. He keeps his portfolio properly allocated, making periodic buys and sells to rebalance the portfolio back to its target allocation. New developments such as exchange traded funds (ETFs) may merit some changes to the investment vehicles from time to time. And there will certainly be a need to change the allocation over time as the investor's needs change. So there is ongoing management, but there is decidedly little *excitement*; it's about as exciting as growing an herb garden.

So you, the investor, must be willing to take your medicine. In this case, the medicine is acceptance of the fact that you will not be *in the game*. You will not be dabbling in biotech stocks. You will not be bragging to your friends that you own the hottest mutual fund on the planet. You will not be flipping money around in commodities. And you will not be featured on "Good Morning America" for the amateur investment club you started that has gained 800% in one year. Instead, you will be the tortoise to their hare in your tidy little well-diversified portfolio, and you will likely earn a lot more than your adrenaline-addicted friends along the way.

Excitement is reserved for those who crave the action. And if action and excitement is what you crave, then my advice is to head to Vegas instead of speculating in the stock market. Your odds of success are about the same, and at least there you'll be entertained while you lose your shirt.

## MYTH 8: Investing Is Exciting

FACT: Investors often fail to grasp the distinction between *speculating* and *investing*. Speculating is exciting and adrenaline-inducing, much like gambling. It can generate much higher short-term returns than prudent investing and also can cause you to lose massive amounts of money. Speculating is not just limited to active traders; people who bet everything on a few stocks or market sectors are also speculating, because their investment fates are not tied to the broad market but to the few market sectors or stocks they have put their money on. In contrast, prudent investing is decidedly unexciting in the short-term, because there is no *action*. It is about making a plan and sticking to it no matter the current market environment.

SOLUTION: Resign yourself to the fact that you aren't going to be "in the game," and learn to tune out the braggadocio of your neighbors who drone on about the hot stock tip they just got from their broker. Remember, when they lose their shirts they won't be coming back to you with a humble accounting of the folly of their ways; they will be hiding in the corner, quietly licking their wounds and mumbling about "the market" while your well-diversified portfolio just keeps trucking along, enjoying the wonders of compound interest over time.

# MYTH 9

## All Risk Is the Same

*"Risk that can be eliminated by adding different stocks (or bonds) is uncompensated risk. The object of diversification is to minimize this uncompensated risk of having too few investments."*
**– excerpt from the Uniform Prudent Investors Act, 1994**

**"Stocks look risky."**

"I'm risk-tolerant."

"I don't want to risk my money in the stock market."

When people get to talking about investing in stocks, the word *risk* is never far behind. This makes sense, because risk is the double-edged sword of investing; it is the reason investors in stocks earn higher returns than bonds or cash deliver, but it is also the reason those same investors can lose their shirts in a bad market.

Historically – going back to 1927 – stocks have delivered an annualized return of 11.4%. Meanwhile, bonds have earned about 7%,

69

and Treasury Bills have returned 3.5%. As we have noted, this excess return stocks have enjoyed above T-Bills is known as the *risk premium*. It is the return investors in stocks have earned for being owners of companies, which carries a lot more risk than being a creditor, which is essentially what bond and cash investors are.

So risk, in this way, is a good thing. On the other hand, it can also be a very *bad* thing, as anyone who has ever owned a stock that went belly-up can attest. Risk is not hypothetical, some sort of magic money maker that you just take more of whenever you want to earn more money. Risk is real.

The real crux of the matter, though, is not so much whether risk is real, but whether risk is *realized*. This is where many investors get themselves into deep – and unnecessary – trouble, because certain types of risk are much more likely to be realized than others.

Wait. Stop. Huh?

Certain *types* of risk? Risk is risk is risk…right?

Au contraire, Pierre. There are many different types of risk, and it is important to know what they are and whether they are worth taking.

This is where investors often get tripped up; if you ask them what they think of when they hear the word risk, they will likely either answer the '29 market crash, Black Monday (October 1987), July 2002 or, more likely these days, the deep market decline that began in the summer of 2007 and accelerated in the fall of 2008 as the credit crisis worsened.

Interestingly, all of the above events are examples of market risk – the risk that is inherent to stock investing. As we said before, it is what makes stock investors their money. You can't earn stock market rates of return in money-market funds. You've got to be in the stock market to get those gaudy gains.

Market risk, then, is a good type of risk. In the investment industry, it is known as *compensated risk,* because you are compensated for risking your money in the stock market in the form of higher returns than you can obtain in bonds and cash investments.

As we noted above, when most investors think of risk, they think of market risk, and it's not hard to understand why: When the broad stock market goes into decline, it gets everyone's attention. Anyone who was invested in stocks during times such as October 2008, when the S&P 500 index dropped more than 20% in just eight trading sessions, can testify that market risk is undeniably real.

On the other hand, market risk is the only type of risk that greatly diminishes over time. Over longer holding periods — ten years is good, twenty or more is great — market risk becomes almost a non-factor. For example, from 1929 through 2006, there were only two ten-year periods when stocks (as measured by the S&P 500) lost money. And there has never been a 20-year run where the stock market ended with a loss.

Even in those two decade-long periods in which the market ended in the red — 1938 and 1939 — the damage was minimal. For example, the ten years ending December 31, 1938, began with the '29 market crash, moved through the Great Depression and culminated with the world on the brink of World War II. When investors go looking for worst-case scenarios in the stock market, those ten years are as bad as they come. And yet the stock market's annual return for that period of time was -0.89%, hardly a devastating decline even during the worst of times — if you stayed put. The ten years ending 1939 was a slight improvement, with the market posting an annual return of -0.51%. And that's it — the rest is good news.

This is where the old "buy-and-hold" adage comes from. If you are (alert! alert!) EFFECTIVELY DIVERSIFIED and have a long time horizon, you can feel extremely confident that market risk is not a big threat to your financial well being.

The same cannot be said for (*ahem*) other types of risk.

For instance, if you were an investor in dot-com stocks in the late 1990s, you took on two huge types of risk that, we know now, had a very high likelihood of being realized. First, you owned the stock of companies that had no intrinsic value and were little more than catchy names being auctioned back and forth in the stock market by frenzied investors looking to get in on the action. This exposed you to a considerable amount of "security risk" – the risk that something goes fundamentally wrong with the individual security (stock) you own, unrelated to the overall stock market. In the case of the dot.com stocks, something *did* go fundamentally wrong – most of them had no real value and, as a result, they blew up.

These investors also had exposed themselves to "sector risk," which comes from being overly concentrated in a certain segment of the stock market, in this case technology stocks. As of 2008, the Nasdaq index was still more than 50% below its 2000 high. Eight years and counting, and it may well be another decade before Nasdaq sees its record high again. These risks – security risk, sector risk – are much more dangerous to investors because they cannot be overcome just by being a buy-and-hold investor. If you applied that sort of discipline to most of the dot-com stocks you would have bought-and-held yourself right into oblivion.

There is another important type of risk that the vast majority of investors take on that often goes unmentioned – manager risk. This is the risk that comes from introducing subjective decision-making into the investment process. If you buy an index fund you have no manager risk, because there is no subjective decision-making involved on the part of the fund – the fund tracks its designated index like an emotionless robot. There is no temptation to makes bets and play hunches because computers can't be tempted. (At least not yet.)

On the other hand, actively managed funds (those that are run by a manager who is charged with beating a market benchmark) carry a huge degree of manager risk. When energy-trading giant Enron suddenly went belly-up in the fall of 2001, it came to light that one of the country's largest mutual funds owned more than 16 million of its shares, representing almost 5% of the fund's assets. Needless to say this was not a welcome bit of news for the fund shareholders. Their frustration only grew, however, when it was learned that the fund manager had actually continued buying the stock all the way until Enron collapsed. By the end of 2001, the fund had registered a 24% decline, almost all of it coming in the fourth quarter.

When pressed about his logic in continuing to buy Enron when such actions seemed completely irrational, the manager famously responded: "All the way down, the stock looked cheap."

*Voila!* Manager risk personified.

Because most investors do not invest in index funds (only 13% of equity mutual fund assets in 2006 went into equity index funds according to the Investment Company Institute), most investors assume some degree of manager risk. And given that over ten-year time periods the vast majority of active managers do not beat their benchmark index, manager risk costs most investors a lot of money.

Recall that market risk is considered to be a form of *compensated risk*, because you can't earn stock market returns without being invested in stocks. In contrast, security risk, sector risk and manager risk are all forms of *uncompensated risk*, because you don't have to assume those risks to earn market rates of return.

So why assume them? Beats me. And yet most investors do just that, taking on risk very imprecisely, failing to grasp the key difference between *good* (compensated) risk and *bad* (uncompensated) risk. They end up with a poorly constructed portfolio that has a great deal of unnecessary volatility, and, when times get tough in the market, they experience losses much greater than what they were emotionally prepared for. Then they flee the market, muttering to themselves about what a horrible investment stocks are.

The goal in putting together a well-constructed portfolio, then, is to diversify away uncompensated risk and only assume as much compensated (market) risk as you need to achieve your goals. So how much risk is that? There is no magic formula, as each individual must balance his need to grow his assets against his ability to sleep at night when the stock market goes into a swoon. An investor who has enough money on which to retire need not take much risk no matter what his ability to tolerate risk is. On the other hand, someone who is a long way from having enough money will need to develop a healthy tolerance of market risk if they expect to earn the kind of returns they will need to build a sizeable nest egg.

This is an important concept to get your arms around. As we have noted, investors should avoid taking on unnecessary volatility, but there is simply no way to diversify away all the risk that comes from stock investing. In 2002, for example, every major equity asset class around the world declined – the first time that had occurred since 1932. Sometimes there is simply no place to hide.

Investors, therefore, must make some peace with the notion of volatility. Think of it as your eccentric Uncle Morty. He drives you crazy. You never know when he's going to show up or how long he's going to stay. When he's around you find it hard to get a good night's sleep. But, ultimately, because you learned to live with him and never ran away from him like all your cousins did, he leaves you a nice inheritance upon his passing. Meanwhile, your short-sighted cousins get bupkis.

Even investors who think they are prudent and have reasonable expectations often lack an understanding of the way volatility works in the market. If I had a nickel for every time an investor has sat across the table from me and said, "I'm not unrealistic about the market; as long as I get 8% every year I'll be happy," – then I'd have, um, a lot of nickels.

The point is that I've heard it a lot, and every time I hear it I cringe, because it reflects a fundamental lack of understanding about the (technical term coming; please remain calm) *variability of returns*. Investors lock onto the well-known tidbit that stocks, over time, have returned around 12% a year. So they decide what their mix of stocks and bonds is going to be, make a guess as to what represents a reasonable return expectation for that mix and then set about waiting to get it. And then, rest assured, they don't get it. Maybe the first year they get a 4%

return. The next year they lose 3%. Then they gain 20%. Then they gain 7%. Then they lose 5%.

This is simply the way the stock market works. Even though the market's long-term average return is, indeed, about 12%, looking back at the 80-year time period from 1927 through 2006, there were only *five years* in which the S&P 500 generated a return of between 10% and 14%, the rest of the returns falling either above or below that range. So while you can reasonably expect that stocks, over time, will likely attain their historical average return, you will only see it in retrospect, looking back over your long holding period. It is highly unlikely that you will obtain anything close to that long-term average return in any given year.

That's why there is so much emphasis on the phrase *long term*. You've got to hang around in the market long enough for that wild, year-by-year roller coaster to average itself out. If you can't afford to ride that roller coaster, then you've got to introduce bonds into the portfolio until you reach a balance between the return you need and the volatility you can stand.

This brings us to what financial planners consider to be the most pressing issue for baby boomers and all those generations that will follow them into retirement. If you are prudently invested, your greatest risk is not losing money in the stock market. Your greatest risk is *outliving your money*. This is a new development, something that has become a reality only in the past two decades or so, and especially in the past few years.

Think about it: Forty years ago, you retired at 65. You got a pension and a social security check. You ate red meat, smoked Pall Malls and watched Walter Cronkite every night for five years. And then you died at age 70. For most retirees, that was pretty much the routine.

Flash forward to today. Workers are retiring earlier than ever – many in their late 50s (and not always voluntarily). Meanwhile, average life expectancy for someone who is 65 years old today is 18 years. Many retirees will live well into their 90s and even beyond, which means that many people will live 20, 30, even *40* years in retirement. Some people will live longer in retirement than they did in their working years! (The good news is, if you believe all those mutual-fund ad campaigns, you will be sky diving and water skiing the whole time.)

Don't let volatility scare you away from the stock market, therefore, because in all likelihood you are going to need the returns that stocks, and only stocks, can provide. Instead, focus on managing risk in your portfolio, ensuring that you are only assuming good forms of risk. And, above all, remember this: *Anything that gets between you and what the stock market is trying to give you is* <u>*bad risk*</u>.

## MYTH 9: All Risk Is the Same

FACT: Most investors fail to distinguish between good risk and bad risk. Good risk can be identified as "market risk," which is the risk that is inherent to stock investing. It's "good" because stock investors receive higher returns than bond and cash investors; investors are compensated for taking on that risk. Bad risk is bad because it is unnecessary to take it; examples of this type of risk include "sector risk," "security risk" and "manager risk." Investors with portfolios concentrated in just a few stocks or market sectors, or who invest in actively managed funds in which fund managers are employing subjective decision making, take on these risks and often pay a heavy price for it.

SOLUTION: Spreading your portfolio across a wide variety of asset classes and investment styles will diversify away most uncompensated risk. Then, decide how much market risk you need (and can stand) based on how much you need to grow your assets to achieve your retirement funding goals. Use index funds and broad-market ETFs to implement your strategy, thereby eliminating manager risk and greatly increasing your net returns compared to actively managed funds.

# MYTH 10

*"It's the end of the world as we know it (and I feel fine)."*
   *– Song from the album* **Document** *by R.E.M., 1987*

**In the past decade** I have noticed a sort of creeping malaise that has come to prevail among many folks, and it seems to be founded in a belief that mankind is headed on a rocket sled down the wrong track. I hear it in fatalistic comments about terrorism, politics, race relations, the environment and religion; many people, it seems, are convinced that things are going from bad to worse and there's no hope in sight. In light of the economic upheaval we experienced in 2008, you may be inclined to agree.

I certainly won't submit that everything is peaches and cream in the world today, or that we can solve all our problems quickly and easily, or even that we *aren't* living in the end times. Obviously I don't know any

79

more than you about things that are inherently unknowable in the present tense.

I do, however, think that the modern-day phenomenon of instantaneous, mass-media communication has played a much bigger role in exaggerating the broken state of the world and increasing the collective pessimism than many of us realize. I also think people underestimate how this constant stream of negativity impacts the way they think, the beliefs they hold and, ultimately, the decisions they make in their daily lives. And, since successful investing requires a healthy sense of confidence and optimism about the future, this malaise mentality makes it exceedingly difficult to be a successful investor. (You thought I was off topic, didn't you?)

No doubt it is easy today to make the case that the world is off its tracks. It would also have been very easy to make such a case in 1963. And in 1942. And in 1929. And in 1913. And in 1862. And in the Middle Ages. And in the Pleistocene Epoch. The truth is, as long as the capital markets have been around, an investor could have easily made a case that the future was bleak and stock investing was folly. And at every turn, investors who let themselves fall prey to such thinking missed out on tremendous growth their assets would have enjoyed had they had a little more faith about the future.

There is not much I envy about our forebears who lived in the centuries before us. Their lives were much shorter and their suffering much greater than what most of us have to endure today. But they had one thing that I do envy, something those of us in the 21st century can never have: Blissful Ignorance. For most folks who lived prior to the 1900s, there was simply very little awareness of events outside their own communities, at least until outside events intruded *into* their communities. Letters and word of mouth were the main source of information. News came in dribs and drabs, usually long after events had run their course. There was little time to sit around and contemplate big-picture issues like whether the polar ice caps are melting and if

Britney Spears can ever find happiness, because no one had any way to know about such things. It left people free to focus on the things that were going on in *their* life – their family, their neighborhood, their town.

Can you imagine what it would have been like if the 24-hour cable news networks had been around a couple of hundred years ago, with all the material they had to work with? The world was more at war than at peace. Millions of people were enslaved. Natural disasters and disease decimated the populace, killing hundreds of thousands every year with no relief from outside agencies or countries. People generally died in their 40s, usually destitute and exhausted. War... Slavery... Famine... Oppression... Disease... Death. A half hour of "Headline News" in those days would have left you cowering in the fetal position under your straw mattress. How hopeless would the fate of man have seemed?

It is no wonder, then, that people today have a sense of despair about the future, because now all the world's problems are reported to us instantly, endlessly, via television and Internet and newspaper and radio and magazine. Problems are beamed to our PDAs in newsflashes. They scroll before our eyes on TVs in restaurants so that we can read about them in case we can't hear them. They are presented to us in clickable format on news websites, categorized and ranked by order of depravity so that we can get to the *very most distressing* problems first, in order to make our day more efficient.

The media thrives on this drama because it gets people to watch, and that is how they make their money. Remember the good old days, when "breaking news" was really breaking news? Now CNN delivers "breaking news" reports about a dozen times an hour, for such dramatic events as a court motion in the Anna Nicole Smith estate trial. And how about "special report?" When I was a kid, a special report from the network usually meant the President was near death or news of similar magnitude. Now Fox News has *an entire daily show* called "Special Report," replete with red banner and dramatic lettering. The media uses these devices because they know we have been conditioned, particularly since 9/11, to look up and pay attention when big news is happening. So they try to make *everything* look like big news, because it keeps us watching.

I am not suggesting that there is anything we can do to stop this situation. Technology has brought us to this point of almost infinite awareness, and we're not going back. Nor am I suggesting that we should turn a blind eye to human suffering, or that it is inherently bad to know about some of these things. We need to know about genocide in Darfur and devastation on the Gulf Coast and the threat of terrorism around the world. We need to know about suffering and injustice and threats to world peace in order to alleviate them.

On the other hand, I don't need to know about a man who was eaten by a Komodo dragon in Indonesia. I am not making this up; I went on the CNN website to find an example of a sensationalistic news item for this chapter and that is the first thing I saw. I am in no way mocking this poor man's demise or the awful way it occurred, but why is this important information for me, sitting half a world away in Atlanta, GA, USA? It is too late to help the poor guy, and last I checked I don't have any Komodo dragons strolling around in my back yard, so why do I need to know about this? Clearly, I don't need to know about it, nor does anyone else who doesn't have to fend off Komodo dragons on a daily basis. It is a news item intended solely for prurient interest, a real-life horror movie that appeals to our morbid curiosity, something that will draw us in and keep us hanging around the web site. The fact is, there are tens of thousands of people who leave this world for the Great Beyond every day, but they aren't reported in the news because their deaths are just so, well... *boring*. One must have a spectacularly awful death to really be newsworthy.

This all goes toward understanding the human psyche. There is simply a limit to how much of this stuff you can digest on a daily basis and still go out in the world with a smile on your face and a song in your heart. To bring this back to an investment perspective, your first challenge as an investor today is to decide how much of the collective calamity you are going to immerse yourself in, and whether you will let it affect your psyche to such an extent that you begin making investment decisions based on the daily parade of distress. It is no coincidence, I think, that trading volumes on the stock exchanges have risen exponentially in the past ten years. Part of that can be attributed to the advent of computers than can handle ever-greater trade volume, but the ability to handle increased capacity doesn't mean that trading has to increase, only that the system can handle it. What has led to the great swell in trading is the hair-trigger mentality so many investors have today, fingers on the mouse button, ready to sell at the slightest sign of trouble, be it economic, political or social. You can almost hear the thoughts running rampant in their heads... "This is it! This is the big one! The market's going to tank – I'm bailing!"

What is missing in all of this pessimism, it seems to me, is a fundamental lack of appreciation for the powerful and dynamic force that is Human Ingenuity. By their very nature, problems haven't been solved yet. But once the world turns its attention to a problem then, more often than not, the problem gets solved. (Remember "Y2K"?) It's not always a clean process, nor a quick one, nor a painless one. But you can trace the problem/solution dynamic back through the history of mankind and see that it is so.

We don't spend a lot of time revisiting old problems and celebrating their solutions, because it's not human nature. We're not wired to look back, but ahead. We could all be sitting around patting ourselves on the back that we don't have to go outside to use the bathroom anymore, but, really – what would be the point?

It is so very important for investors in today's world to have some perspective about this, because investing at its core is about *optimism*. If you're going to be a successful investor, you've got to have some faith in your fellow man. You've got to have perspective on the reality that problems are inherent to human existence, and have some faith in our ability to ultimately provide a solution to those problems, even when none seems present. Personally, I stopped watching the cable news networks and reading their websites altogether shortly after 9/11, because I found it impossible to relax. All of this information flowing in from all over the world, all of it distressing, with almost no filter, being force fed into my brain all day long. It was simply overwhelming to my senses. So I stopped playing the game. I quit watching the news when I got home. I changed my home page on my web browser to a financial site that does not report any non-financial news. I let my *Newsweek* subscription lapse.

Maybe you think I'm just sticking my head in the sand and pretending the problems will go away, but that's not it at all. The news still gets through to me today more than it ever did ten years ago. Every time I check my Hotmail account I see the headlines on MSN. Every time I pick up *The Wall Street Journal* to read the investing section I see the news summary on the front page. When I watch a ballgame on TV at night my local affiliate jams the upcoming news down my throat in ten seconds whether I want it or not. So when an issue of importance or interest to me pops up I check into it. I don't feel out of the loop at all; I just don't swim in the depravity all day long.

You'd be surprised how big a difference it makes in your perspective about reality. And how much more money it makes you as an investor.

## MYTH 10: The End Is Near – So Why Invest?

FACT: The sensitivity of investors to bad news and fear of future events is exponentially greater today than it was in years past. Much of this is attributable to the endless, instantaneous transmission of news, which is distressing and overwhelming to the senses. The advent of electronic trading has enabled investors to trade on these fears and anxieties at a moment's notice. Your opinion about the state of the world, where we are headed and how fast we are headed there is a matter of personal perspective, but if you let negativity start influencing your investment decisions then you are *guaranteeing* a bleak future (at least financially) for yourself.

SOLUTION: Consider generations past and realize how easy it would have been to let the state of the world keep you from being a confident investor and what the cost of that negativity would have been. Muster some faith in the future and in mankind's ability to solve problems that in the present are, by definition, unsolved. If you can't find that faith, then, quite honestly, you should not be invested in the stock market.

# MYTH 11

## I'm Not a Market Timer

*"Don't try to buy at the bottom and sell at the top. It can't be done except by liars."*

**– Famed Wall Street financier Bernard M. Baruch (1870-1965)**

*Welcome!*

*I'm glad you could make it to our meeting. Please have a seat over there in one of the folding chairs.*

*I want you to know that you aren't going to be judged by anyone in this room, okay? You're among friends here. You're in a safe place and can speak freely without guilt or shame.*

*Now, tell us: How long have you been a market timer?*

*Wait! Don't get up! You didn't know this was an MTA meeting – Market Timers Anonymous? You say you don't need any help because you're NOT a market timer?*

*Uh, oh… Denial. We've got a long way to go here…*

Perhaps you are one of the few investors out there who's never given into the urge to change their investment strategy according to short-term market conditions. Maybe you didn't buy a tech fund in 1999. Perhaps you didn't leave any cash sitting on the sidelines after 9/11 and just plowed that money right into the stock market, brimming with confidence and serenity.

If so, please accept this:

> ### *Official Permission Slip*
> ### *to Skip This Chapter*

Now, for the rest of us – let's explore this horrible addiction investors have to market timing and its devastating financial consequences.

The first hurdle to get over is denial. When most people hear the phrase "market timer," they envision some nerdy guy with horned-rimmed glasses who spends all day looking at stochastic charts of the stock market's historical performance, extolling the virtues of the strategy he has discovered for exploiting the market cycles that he calls "Head and Shoulders Tops" (which, for, the record, I am not making up). The guy probably publishes a newsletter for which he charges a cool $300 a year to share his insight into how you, too, can profit from his foolproof market-timing theory. (Step 1: Get a theory and then get a bunch of people to pay you $300 for your newsletter...)

Now, if you receive a complimentary copy of this newsletter in your mailbox, you would probably say something like "pshaw!" (I said "something *like*"). You are smart enough to know that market timing doesn't work. You've read plenty of articles, even in the mainstream press, that say as much. And you know a carnival barker when you see one, which Mr. Market Timer in the newsletter clearly is. This is not for you. After all, you are almost always a DISCIPLINED, BUY-AND-HOLD INVESTOR!

Alas, it is that "almost always" that really gets investors into trouble...

Most investors behave pretty rationally most of the time, because most of the time the market behaves pretty rationally. Stocks go up like they are supposed to. Downturns come and go fairly quickly. It's easy to be disciplined when you're making money, because it's not really discipline at all. It's like saying you are a disciplined eater of ice cream.

But from time to time, the market loses its bearing in a major way. The whole financial system seems to come unglued, as if the free-market model just doesn't work any more. Those are times of malaise, crisis and sometimes even panic, as we saw in 1929, 1974, 1987, 1998, 2002 and, at the time of this writing, 2007-08. Those are the days when being a long-term investor is not such a sanguine experience. Not coincidentally, those are also the days when many investors blink.

The "blink moment" usually comes during the height of the market turmoil, when trading volume on the exchanges swells five times its normal amount, the market experiences wild gyrations, and the media is in wall-to-wall crisis coverage mode. Emotion – fear, specifically – reigns supreme on Wall Street. This is when John Q. Investor gets a look at his online balance and realizes he has lost a lot of money. And then comes the next step in the thought progression, the inevitable one, the one the media puts in his head every time he turns on the TV or opens the paper:

"What if this continues? What if it all falls apart? What if I lose...*everything???*"

*Blink!*

John Q. Investor sells his positions and heads for the perceived safety of a money-market fund. "Just for awhile," he tells himself. "Just until the stock market regains its senses." Deep down, a nagging voice tells Mr. Investor he's made a knee-jerk emotional decision. But he just *feels* better now that he's not losing any sleep about the market.

Mr. Investor, however, has only made the first part of a two-part decision that all market timers face, and it is often the easier of the two – getting out. Now he faces an even greater dilemma, one that will not reveal itself all at once but that will slowly gnaw at him like termites in the foundation in the weeks, months and even years ahead:

*When to get back in.*

Investors who are unable to resist the urge to flee the market imagine there will be some magical point in time, some clarion call in the future, when the clouds part and Adam Smith comes down from the Great Beyond riding an Invisible Hand and proclaiming that now – NOW! – is the time to get back in the market.

If only it were so. The reality is that such moments of clarity never present themselves to the investor who is sitting on the sidelines. If the market continues to go down, well…he's not getting back in the market *now*, not with his money safely tucked away in cash investments while all those fools are still losing money in stocks. And if, as often happens, the market shoots up rapidly and unexpectedly, then he's *definitely* not getting back in, not when stocks are so logically due for a fall. He'll wait until the market drops and then get back in, he assures himself. Except that if the market drops he won't want to get back in for fear it's going to drop even more, and if the market continues to climb he will be *absolutely sure* that it's going to drop now, since it's been going up for so long. Thus does the market timer end up on the sidelines for months or even years, stuck in an endless loop, paralyzed and even more nauseous about what to do than he was when he made the decision to get out of the market.

Perhaps as you read this you are saying to yourself, "He's not preaching to me. I've never bailed out of the market. No way I would do that." If so, then I congratulate you on your intestinal fortitude. But I would also challenge you to look at your past behavior and see if there are not, in fact, some instances in which you allowed short-term market conditions to influence your investment decisions. For while market timing at its most extreme is about moving entirely out of the market, it is an affliction that comes in many forms, and rare is the investor who has not contracted it. Shifting money from growth to value, or from foreign to domestic, or from technology to health care, or even from a bad fund to a hot fund – all of these are forms of market timing, instances in which investors are seeking to be ahead of where the market is going or seeking to get away from where the pain is being incurred.

In recent years Wall Street, in its endearing way, has greatly enhanced the ability of individual investors to engage in market timing by rolling out dozens and dozens of exchange-traded funds covering ridiculously narrow market sectors. In theory, ETFs make great investment vehicles when used to track broad market indexes or specific investment styles like growth or value, because they provide broad market exposure very cheaply and with great tax efficiency.

But now ETFs are being sliced-and-diced into narrow sectors, such as energy, financials, health care, and sometimes even down to tiny, bizarre sub-sectors such as "emerging cancer." (Don't ask me – I don't own it.) The brokerage industry encourages investors to flip these ETFs frequently, "overweighting" one and "underweighting" another based on their "proprietary research" models. Thus do we now have legions of investors using ETFs like betting chips on the craps table, placing their money on, say, consumer staples, blowing on the dice and whispering "C'mon baby!" under their breath.

Vanguard founder John Bogle, the grandfather of the index fund, took the brokerage industry to task for its abuse of the ETF concept in a February 9, 2007, article in *The Wall Street Journal*:

*These nouveau index funds starkly contradict each of the principal concepts underlying the original index fund. If the broadest possible diversification was the original paradigm, surely holding small segments of the market offers less diversification and commensurately more risk. If the original paradigm was minimal cost, then holding market-sector index funds that may themselves be low-cost obviates neither the brokerage commissions entailed in trading them nor the tax burdens incurred if one has the good fortune to do so successfully.*

*In addition to the certain penalty of expenses, there is the less certain – but omnipresent – penalty of emotions. Performance-chasing investors in specialized funds are their own worst enemies. The most rapidly growing sectors of the ETF marketplace are those – no surprise – that have been the leaders in the recent bull market: indexes of small-cap stocks, energy, emerging markets, international, real estate and, most recently, commodities (especially gold and oil). The annualized share turnover of these sectors averages an astonishing 2500%.*[20]

Few investors who engage in such activity believe themselves to be market timers; they just think they are being smart by following whatever market sector has been hot lately. But as we have noted, and despite what Wall Street wants you to believe, there is zero relevance between what has been hot and what will be hot going forward. None. Not even a little.

It is ironic that today we have so many ways to divert ourselves from the very simple, straightforward path to investment success. There are now, for example, almost as many mutual funds in the marketplace as there are individual stocks! Investors today are the proverbial kids in the candy store, except that in this case the candy store is being run by Wall Street, and the kids are lying on the floor writhing with stomach cramps because they have had so much junk shoved down their throats. Investors need a lot less sugar and a lot more fiber. They need to quit playing around with all the sexy toys Wall Street rolls out on a daily basis and quit following its implicit encouragement to *move! move! move!* their money around on a semi-daily basis. They need to be honest with themselves about the perils of market timing and resolve to be in the market, in a sound strategy, all the time, no matter what.

So what exactly constitutes a sound strategy? I'm glad you asked...

It is true that there are just about as many investment strategies out there as there are investments themselves, and any of them can sound tempting if the salesman who's pitching it is talented enough. But did you know there's only one established investment strategy that has actually won a Nobel Prize in Economic Science? That strategy, known as Modern Portfolio Theory (MPT), was established by three of the 20th century's leading thinkers in financial markets analysis: Harry Markowitz, Merton Miller and William Sharpe, all of whom shared the Nobel Prize in 1990 for their efforts.

Why such high accolades for an investment theory? Quite simply, MPT fundamentally changed the understanding of what prudent investment management really means. According to MPT, asset classes and investment styles (such as growth and value, large and small, foreign and domestic, etc.) should be combined in a portfolio with an understanding of the effect those asset classes have on each other, not just evaluated on their own. For example, large U.S. growth stocks and REIT (real estate) stocks each have a high degree of volatility on their own, but when they are combined in a portfolio they actually help *reduce* the portfolio's volatility. This is because those two asset classes historically have a low correlation relative to one another; when large growth stocks are in favor, REIT stocks tend to be out of favor, and vice versa.

In the 1970s and '80s, MPT opened the door for large institutional investors such as pension plans, endowments and foundations to greatly improve the diversification of their investment portfolios. No longer was a volatile asset class considered imprudent (and thus a breach of fiduciary responsibility) if that asset class played a role in reducing the overall volatility of the portfolio. Then, in the 1990s, MPT made its way from the institutional ranks and began to be embraced by a devoted following of investment advisors, many of whom had grown frustrated with the fruitless quest of "chasing returns" from one hot mutual fund to another and saw the great logic in constructing disciplined portfolios based on asset-class correlations, not recent performance history.

Today, MPT is the gold-standard for prudent investment management, whether for large institutional investors or individuals. In fact, it was the explicit underpinning of the Uniform Prudent Investors Act, which sets the guidelines for prudent fiduciary conduct in most states. While nearly everyone in the investment industry today touts the virtues of "diversification," the measure of that commitment is whether the investment professional is truly adhering to the principles of Modern Portfolio Theory.

I do not assert that MPT is some sort of panacea, a free pass around the volatility that, as we have noted, is an inherent part of stock investing. To be sure, there are times such as 2002 and 2008 when nearly every equity asset class goes into a freefall and there is no short-term benefit to be had from diversification. What MPT does accomplish with spectacular results is to *eliminate the risk of bad guessing* in your investment portfolio. There is no guessing that large cap stocks are the place to be, or that now is a good time to get in or out of the market, and then finding out the hard way the dire consequences of guessing wrong. By combining a wide variety of asset classes and investment styles together in our portfolio, we are hedging our bets about the near-term fate of any one segment of the market and accomplishing our goal of letting the capital markets work for us.

Following the principles of MPT gives you a much more sanguine investment experience, even during periods of turmoil, because you are not making moves that you *hope* will turn out right. MPT allows you to stay put regardless of what the market does, and that alleviates the considerable anxiety that comes from wondering if you have made the right move at the right time with your assets. You'd be amazed at how freeing it is, even when the market is in a steep decline, to do absolutely nothing with your investment strategy due to short-term market conditions.

Give it a try.

## MYTH 11: I'm Not a Market Timer

FACT: Few investors have the steely resolve necessary to stay the course in a prudent strategy, all the time, in every market environment. At some point in their investment lives, most individuals will allow current events to influence their investment decisions, a deviation that will result in lost future earnings for the investor.

SOLUTION: Follow the tenets of Modern Portfolio Theory to develop a prudently diversified portfolio suitable to your risk and return needs. Once you are invested in a sound strategy, you must recognize the danger in making short-term alterations to your investments *no matter how sensible they may seem in the heat of the moment.*

# MYTH 12

An Investment Advisor's Job Is to Find You "Opportunities"

*"No, but I play one on TV!"*

*— Response from a stockbroker when asked by an*
*undercover reporter from* **SmartMoney** *magazine*
*if he acted as a fiduciary on behalf of his clients.*

**It is widely perceived** by investors, and promoted by the brokerage industry, that the primary role of an investment advisor is to bring you "opportunities." To scour the world of investments and bring before you only the choicest offerings, things that the Average Joe would never be privy to, but that you, lucky soul that you are, now have a chance to get in on. (Note: If the phrase "ground floor opportunity" is uttered, you might as well just empty your wallet on the table and walk out the door. It will save you some time.)

This notion of being given access to special opportunities appeals to the ego of the investor, and thus it is an easy sell for the broker. But I ask you to consider this: How often do ego-based decisions work out for you? (If you are Donald Trump, please sit this one out.) Ego-based decisions are emotional decisions, and, as we have noted, it is emotions that get investors in trouble every time.

That, then, begs the question: What *is* the primary role of an investment advisor?

As seems to be the case with most chapters in this book, the answer is a lot less exciting than you probably want to hear. But my mission here is to spread the truth and debunk myth, whatever the consequences, so here goes:

*The primary role of an advisor is to bring objectivity, discipline and calm resolve to the investment process, so that emotion and guesswork are removed from the equation.*

*ZZZZZZZZZZZZZ.*

I know. It's a snoozer. It sounds a lot less compelling than the guy who is selling you on the dream of finding the next Microsoft. It's like your mother is making you eat lima beans when your buddy next to you is shotgunning Pixie Sticks.

And yet, if you will recall, *there was a very good reason* your mother made you eat your vegetables and wouldn't permit you the fleeting pleasure of mainlining colored sugar no matter how good it tasted in the moment. It was the right thing to do. It was the best thing for you. Your long-term health depended on it.

This, then, is what being a good investment advisor is all about. Being a doting parent and keeping the kids – er, clients – on the right path and out of trouble. Patronizing? Simplistic? Maybe. But true nonetheless. In many respects, the most important thing an investment advisor can do for you is get between your money and your emotions, because that is when investors do the real damage to their portfolios.

Unfortunately, the vast majority of people who make their living in the investment industry fail to grasp this key concept and, very often, encourage the opposite mindset.

Here is a great litmus test: If you called up your advisor in late 1999 and asked him or her to "get you in on some of this tech stock action," what was the answer? If it was, "Sure, we can do that!", then you didn't have an advisor, you had a facilitator, a yes-person who didn't want to tackle the unpleasantries of trying to convince you that it was a bad idea to buy something that had tripled in price in about six weeks, despite the fact that your neighbor mortgaged his house to buy the same and had just jetted off for a vacation in Monte Carlo. (And if your advisor called *you* trying to sell you some tech stocks, then you didn't even have a facilitator; you just had a snake-oil salesman.)

Those are difficult conversations for advisors, because they require the fortitude of telling clients to do something that flies in the face of all the clients think they know to be true. Personally, I can recall how unnerving it was trying to convince clients not to pile into tech stocks during this time, because I didn't know for sure how long the madness would persist. It seemed as if all the known laws of the universe governing the way markets work had been suspended, and free money was being made by everyone. Of course, this was the *exact reason* I was telling clients not to invest in tech stocks, but I didn't pretend to know where we were going or when the day of reckoning would come. What if it was ten more years of this? What if it really was a "new era" in which such stodgy old fundamentals as "earnings" were irrelevant? It seems so obvious today that we were in a speculative market bubble, but it sure wasn't back then. It was hard not knowing if your clients were going to be the only ones who weren't billionaires by the end of 2000.

*But this is exactly what I was being paid for:* To be the impartial, emotionless advisor who kept telling my clients what I knew, fundamentally, was the right thing to do, which was to avoid chasing hot performance no matter what is going on in the world around you. Even if – *especially if* – your neighbor who drives a delivery truck is now off tanning in Monte Carlo.

It is hard to underestimate the real value that a true advisor brings to a client, because the real dollars earned, and losses avoided, come from keeping clients on the straight-and-narrow path. In the grand scheme, this is much more important than whether an advisor recommends Growth Fund A or Growth Fund B.

Here's a real-life example: In February 2000, a prospective client came to me and asked that I evaluate her portfolio. She had approximately $500,000 that was concentrated in a half-dozen growth and technology mutual funds. Needless to say she had enjoyed some dramatic gains in those funds in 1998 and '99. I told her she should sell them.

"Why?" she asked, in the same way you would ask if someone told you to stop making so much money.

"Because you have a lot of risk in such a concentrated portfolio," I told her. "You could wake up and have half these assets in a very short period of time."

I had no way of knowing at that time that we were on the eve of the worst market decline since the Great Depression. I only knew that she was taking on unnecessary risk for her needs *even though she had benefitted from taking that risk.* As with many prospects in those days, I fully expected her to call me a sissy and storm out the door. (Technically no one ever called me a sissy, but I could see it in their eyes...)

But she didn't. This particular prospect was a smart, level-headed woman who knew what I was saying was true. She quickly realized that she could not afford the potential downside of such a volatile portfolio no matter how fabulous the upside might have been. So she hired me and we set about selling all those technology funds with all their embedded capital gains and reinvested her in a diversified portfolio that had generated returns of less than half of what she had enjoyed the prior three years. It was, shall we say, an exercise in faith.

Then, almost immediately, the bubble burst. Within days after we moved this client into a more prudent, diversified portfolio, technology stocks began a deep descent from which they have yet to emerge. By the end of 2003, the investment portfolio that we had placed her in had enjoyed some reasonable gains – nothing spectacular, but certainly a moral victory in a terrible market environment. On the other hand, had she remained in her portfolio of technology funds, she would have lost around 60% of her wealth.

My value to the client was not as a "finder of opportunities." My value was in playing the role of a true *advisor*, looking her in the eye and telling her to get out a risky investment portfolio even though I had no way of knowing if my advice would prove right, at least not any time soon. And because I acted as the boring, emotionless android that a good advisor is supposed to be, I kept this client from losing, as it turns out, more than half her money.

It's not that I am so smart; any advisor who truly understands this mission did the same during the technology stock bubble. Alas, a great many investment professionals fail to understand the critical distinction between being an advisor and a facilitator. At my firm, we have a program in which we partner with accounting firms who want to offer investment advisory services to their clients. In this program, the accounting firms handle the client relationships and we manage the money. Because accountants are fairly new to my industry, we spend a great deal of time training them on the nuances of being a good investment advisor, and this distinction between advisor and facilitator is often a struggle for them. Like other service professions, accounting is about bringing information to the client and helping that client make an informed decision. When a client calls up and says they need the accountant to do something for them, the CPA, being a good service professional, does the job in a timely, professional manner. After all, that's what service *is*.

This is a real challenge for an investment advisor, because when it comes to investing, what clients "want" is very often a knee-jerk reaction to short-term market events and is therefore likely the worst thing they can do. Following an investor's wishes in such circumstances, at least without a spirited debate, basically makes such an advisor the Dr. Kevorkian of financial suicide. In times of market extremes, when emotions run rampant, what investors need is a calm, steady demeanor and a healthy dose of intestinal fortitude. *That* is what will make clients money over the long term, because it will keep them invested.

The brokerage industry hates this mindset; it lives both for the scorching-hot market rallies and the gut-wrenching market declines, because that is when investors get emotional and want help. Only "help" is not what is being offered. Brokerage firms see these times of market extremes as opportunities to move product and, in a perverse sort of way, they don't really care whether the market is really good or really bad, because they can package their product-moving schemes to look like solutions in either market environment. In roaring bull markets such as we saw in the late '90s, the brokers position themselves as the magical investment sherpa who guides the investor to secret opportunities in the land of financial Shangri-La. Then, in times of deep declines, they sell themselves as the omniscient, omnipotent trader who deftly moves clients to the side just as a market correction sets in and then moves them back when the danger has passed.

Investors want to believe this, and the firms are happy to sell them the myth. And that's exactly what it is, because there is no free pass in the stock market; if you are attaining a certain amount of reward in the form of high returns, then rest assured you are taking on an amount of risk commensurate with that return.

It's not like this is a big secret in the investment industry. So the question for the investment professional really is this: *Just how cynical are you?* Are you going to be a salesman, pitching the investor on hot performance, knowing full well you probably won't deliver it? Or are you going to be a true advisor, educating the investor about why such a tempting approach doesn't work and probably having a lot less success, on the front end at least, than the guy selling performance?

Here the road diverges in the investment industry. The road more traveled is the sales path, selling the dream of hot performance. It is the path more taken because it results in bang-up sales numbers. It also results in nearly 100% client turnover over time, because clients don't get what they are promised (outsized returns) and the broker doesn't bother to service them because he knows they won't be happy anyway and he doesn't want to have to deal with unhappy clients and, besides, he's got sales to make, what with all his clients leaving all the time. (I call this the "Scorched Earth Approach.")

The path less taken is the advisor who tells it like it is and builds a base of loyal clients who have been well informed about what the advisor can and cannot do. The advisor who will look you in the eye in times of turmoil and say "Stay!" The advisor who will harangue you when you ask him to buy you a high-flying stock even though all your buddies are doing it.

There is no magic being sold; the advisor is judged solely on the merits of his counsel and his service. It ain't easy – the success rate in bringing in new clients will be far lower than the performance hawker who takes the easy road.

But you sure do sleep better at night.

## MYTH 12: An Investment Advisor's Job Is to Find You "Opportunities"

FACT: By far, the most important role of an investment advisor is to bring discipline and resolve to the investment process and provide a barrier between your money and your emotions. "Advisors" who are constantly peppering you with the latest, greatest investment opportunity – be it fund, manager, stock , annuity, or whatever – are not advisors at all but merely product sellers in sheep's clothing.

SOLUTION: Find an independent, fee-only advisor who receives no compensation from any investment he or she recommends. This alone doesn't guarantee competency, but it does at least guarantee objectivity.

# CONCLUSION

*"I know people who have a lot of money and they get testimonial dinners and hospital wings named after them. But the truth is that nobody in the world loves them. When you get to my age, you'll measure your success in life by how many of the people you want to have love you actually do love you. That's the ultimate test of how you've lived your life."*

– **Warren Buffett, as quoted in Parade *magazine, September 7, 2008***

**If you've read this** much of this book, you're obviously a smart, motivated person. (Go with it – it makes us both feel good.) You probably know a good bit more than the average bear about how to make smart decisions with your money, and now, hopefully, you have a clear understanding of the fundamentals of successful investing. You could follow the principles I have outlined in this book and use them to create a significant amount of wealth for yourself and your family.

But that is only the beginning, not the end. Typically the *acquisition* of wealth – whether by disciplined saving, inheritance, stock options, selling a business or winning the lottery – is where most people devote their planning efforts. Investors spend considerable time and effort focusing on how much they will need to sustain them in retirement, running scenarios, making detailed plans, checking and rechecking assumptions, implementing investment strategies to get them to those goals, and then monitoring their progress as they set out on their quest for financial security.

The interesting part is what happens once those goals are reached, for when that day does come, few are prepared for the new and very different challenges that wealth brings. At my firm we have an investment minimum of $2 million, which means that a lot of people with a lot of money pass through my office in any given year. And over the years I have noticed a curious thing: *A surprising number of people who have a lot of money are not very happy.*

I know, I know. "Cry me a river!" you say. And yet it's true: Managing wealth becomes a slippery slope for families, and much of the trouble can be attributed to a fundamental lack of appreciation for the sheer cosmic power of money. It is a story as old as time immemorial, and yet one that goes largely unheeded. Money is not just currency; it is a life force, an energy field. It is fissile material. Properly handled, it can be a tool of great construction; in the wrong hands, it is a tool of personal destruction with a half-life that spans generations. Far too often, people become slavishly devoted to the accumulation of money and give no thought as to what they are going to do and who they are going to be when they *get there*, the place where they have money and lots of it. And that is where the trouble begins, for managing wealth is not a rote exercise like doing your taxes or writing a letter or changing your oil. It is a challenge to the soul, a task infused with every human emotion. Think of the Seven Deadly Sins: Pride. Lust. Greed. Wrath. Envy. Sloth. Gluttony. In many respects, money touches them all.

Successfully managing wealth, therefore, is about proactive planning and stewardship. It is about overcoming emotion, temptation and base human instinct and guiding your wealth in a patient, prudent manner. It means getting wills in order, trusts set up and insurance policies in place, but it is also more than that. It requires exploring your fundamental values, immersing yourself in a level of introspection to which people are often not inclined. When we are in our wealth accumulation years, such introspection often feels pretentious; we may permit ourselves to participate in the occasional "visioning" exercise about how we would handle significant wealth, but it rings hollow. Deep down there is a voice telling us, "First let's get the $10 million. *Then* we'll figure out how to handle it."

The funny thing is, once you *do* get the $10 million, you are exponentially less likely to want to spend that time thinking about what you want to do with your wealth. Suddenly, everything is a possibility; pleasurable diversions abound. Who wants to spend a lot time pondering thorny issues, like how to share the blessings of your wealth with your children and grandchildren without depriving them of the fundamental need to be productive human beings striving to reach their potential? Or planning for how you will do the same for yourself even when you have enough money to sit around and watch The Price Is Right all day if you bloody well want to?

Solving these challenges doesn't just happen. To the contrary, it is far easier for the *opposite* to happen – to let the siren song of wealth lull you into a complacency with the status quo, believing that all is well because the large balance in your brokerage account makes you feel it is so. If you need something, you buy it. If you have a problem, you fix it. What's so hard about that?

Underneath the placid surface, though, trouble is percolating, and often times it doesn't boil over for many years. Then, suddenly, you are faced with the consequences of your lack of proactive planning and attention to managing money instead of letting it manage you. We have all heard the stories of families divided and embittered because of the division of inheritance. Grown children who are stumbling through life without a purpose because all their material needs were met and all their problems were solved for them. Widowed spouses who lose millions of dollars to unscrupulous advisors because they were suddenly thrust into having to deal with financial issues for which they were unprepared. Entrepreneurs who lose everything they spent their lives working for because their personal assets weren't properly sheltered against litigants. Faced with such crises, families often crumble under the weight. Many have said they would have been better off had they never had all that money in the first place.

In many ways, then, managing wealth brings on a series of ongoing issues that are even more challenging than creating wealth. You are no longer of a singular focus (making money). Now your challenges are diffuse and ever-morphing.

The good news is that these are challenges that can be met very successfully with proper planning and introspection. And this leads to a critical decision on your part: Are you going to commit to managing your wealth – not just your investments, but all aspects of your financial life – as though it were your vocation? Not just a job, but something that you embrace with passion and enthusiasm? The wealthy individuals I have seen successfully manage their own wealth approach it in this manner. It becomes paramount to them to get their financial house in order and *keep* it in order over time, as things change in their life and the lives of their family. Planning becomes a living thing, not something they do one time and file away in a safe-deposit box.

Such an effort requires coordination between a number of experts from a variety of fields: estate-planning attorneys, insurance experts, accountants and, obviously, investment experts. All parties should work together as a united team, with a thorough understanding of your needs, values and desires and – importantly – a thorough understanding of what each member of that expert team is doing for you. The plan that team develops for you will be your blueprint for how you take the wealth you have been blessed with and nurture it over time to achieve the things that are important to you. Just as importantly, this plan also helps ensure that you avoid the kind of tragic outcomes that often befall wealthy families because of a lack planning and guidance.

If you don't have the passion and enthusiasm to be the guiding force in this effort, then you need to find a wealth manager who will do that for you. And here you must be careful, because the term "wealth manager" has been cribbed by just about everyone in the investment industry who has any kind of securities license. Look under the hood of whomever you seek to help you in this regard and ensure that they meet the following four criteria:

**1.  Objectivity:** The wealth manager should be an independent firm, free of any conflicts of interest or product compensation.

**2.  Sound Investment Philosophy:** A wealth management plan can very quickly be undone by a poor investment philosophy. The investment strategy should be based on the principles of Modern Portfolio Theory and demonstrate a disciplined adherence to those principles.

**3.  Expertise:** A good wealth management firm should have demonstrated expertise in investment counsel and financial planning. Also consider the length of time the firm has been in business and the firm's reputation in the marketplace.

**4.  Relationship Management:** Wealth management is a complex undertaking, and no one advisor possesses all of the expertise in all areas. A capable wealth manager should have a team that includes attorneys, accountants and insurance experts, all of whom work together to develop a coordinated plan for you that addresses a wide range of issues, including wealth management, wealth protection, wealth transfer and charitable giving.

It sounds like a lot to consider, I know, but devoting some time on the front end to this pursuit may be the most important undertaking of your life, even more than when you were *amassing* your wealth. It will ensure that you accomplish the thing that most people think is easy when you have a lot of money, and yet it is the very thing that most wealthy people will tell you is most elusive:

*Peace of mind.*